A HIGH SCHOOL
PARENT'S GUIDE
TO
COLLEGE SUCCESS

12 ESSENTIALS

BY
AMY BALDWIN AND BRIAN TIETJE

Dedications

I dedicate this book to all the hard-working parents who want the best for their offspring and all the teachers, professors, counselors, advisors, coaches, mentors, tutors, and group leaders who dedicate every day to helping support students and their development into successful adults.

— Amy Baldwin

To my Lord who saved me; Debbie, whose love inspires me; my parents, who sacrificed for me; and Summer and Hunter, who make parenting the greatest privilege I have ever known.

— Brian Tietje

Acknowledgements

No book comes to fruition without the help and guidance of many people. We know we will most likely omit someone in this list, but we will do our best.

For the edits and feedback, thank you Jennifer Gessner. Your expert eye and probing questions led us to several, much-needed changes. We also appreciate the quick, intuitive work of Tatiana Fernandez on the cover design and Brian Schwartz and his amazing platform Author Dock to keep us organized during the process. Lesley Curtis and Lisa Carver with Studio Muse have worked diligently on getting the word out about this book. Thank you for helping us expand our vision of who needs to read this book and thank you for the assistance in reaching many more readers.

People in our lives come and go, but all have made an enormous impact on our ability to complete this project. Thank you to our co-collaborators Laurie Hazard and Stephanie Carter, whose own book *Your Freshman Is Off to College* gave us the impetus to get our ideas into parents' hands; we appreciate your guidance, late-night calls and texts, and general congeniality. It helps knowing we are all working toward the same goal. We would be remiss if we did not pay tribute to the editors who started us on this path: Sande Johnson, Jodi McPherson, and Paul Smith have, each in their own time and way, influenced us and were instrumental in building the path that has led us to where we are now. Thank you.

Website and design support has been crucial to sharing our ideas with other parents and professionals. Thank you, Nina Rodriguez, Kristen Dang, Elaine Sullivan, for your work on crafting our online presence. You have been responsive, imaginative, and helpful!

Our professional lives are as rich with creative, innovative, and supportive people as our personal lives are. Thank you to the University of Central Arkansas for being an institution that believes in student success. Thank you to my (Amy's) tireless colleagues Penny Hatfield, Julia Winden Fey, Courtney Bryant, Kurt Boniecki, and Kathy Wages who have helped me in ways they may never fully realize, but most definitely as partners in the crime of helping students succeed. Thank you to Cal Poly, for being my (Brian's) home and source of pride and fulfillment for my entire academic career.

Our respective families deserve acknowledgement for their continued love and support while we committed our ideas to paper. Thank you to Kyle, Emily, and Will (Baldwin) who pursued their own interests so I (Amy) could spend weekends and evenings writing. You are all quite tolerant of my writing (and reading) addiction. Thank you, Debbie, Summer, and Hunter (Tietje) for inspiring and supporting me (Brian) as I embarked on this journey of authorship.

We are fortunate and blessed to have a wonderful community of family, friends, and colleagues who believe in us and our work. This book—and the positive impact we hope it has on parents and their students—is a collaborative outcome that we are grateful to share with all of you.

About the Authors

AMY BALDWIN, Ed.D., is a renowned educator and educational entrepreneur. She wrote the first, groundbreaking student success textbook for community colleges and for first-generation students. Because of her work with national initiatives such as Complete College America, Achieving the Dream, and the Developmental Education Initiative, she has become a sought-after keynote speaker and workshop facilitator on student success topics. After 18 years as an award-winning community college professor, she now serves as Director of University College at the University of Central Arkansas. Amy and her husband Kyle live in central Arkansas with their two young adults Emily and Will.

BRIAN TIETJE, Ph.D., is Vice Provost of International, Graduate and Extended Education at Cal Poly in San Luis Obispo, California. He is a thought leader in higher education and a passionate advocate for student success, particularly for those who face challenging circumstances and who may not be familiar with the unwritten rules of college and career success. Brian took his life experiences and determination from rural Ohio cross-country as he traversed educational and corporate ladders to reach an executive leadership position in higher education. He held previous leadership roles as the Dean of Extended Education, and the Associate Dean and Director of Graduate Programs in the Orfalea College of Business. He is also a Professor of Marketing and has been a member of the Cal Poly faculty since 1999. Brian and his wife, Debbie, live on the Central Coast of California with their daughter, Summer, and son, Hunter.

Table of Contents

Introduction

Are You College Ready? Is Your Student?

If you read the headlines and listen to the news, you will believe that every parent of a high school student is nervous, anxious, and a bit worried about his student's future. If the worry isn't how to get into one of those coveted *U.S. News & World Report*'s best colleges and universities, then it is anxiety over how to pay for the ever-rising costs of college without going into bankruptcy. And then there is the nervousness about the student's readiness to be on her own, navigate the new social and academic realms, and act as an emerging adult. Quite honestly, just thinking about it all can be overwhelming. What can you do to help your high school student get better prepared to face those challenges? How can you ensure that at the very least, you and your student are college ready?

The good news is that you *can* do something now. With our combined experience of over 40 years of teaching and administration in both community colleges and universities, we have seen what students need to know and what students need to do to be successful in college, and those habits can be developed years before they set foot on a college campus. Our book *A High School Parent's Guide to College Success: 12 Essentials* provides parents like you with the information and tools to get your student ready for the challenges and opportunities that college will offer. We break down the basic skills and habits that are needed for students to start strong; we provide strategies for parents to help their students develop those skills and habits; and we provide the inside track for being successful in college and after graduation.

The Essentials We Chose...and Why 12?

Whenever constructing a list of important qualities or traits, there's always a question of how long that list should be. When thinking about what it takes to be a successful college student, we tended to think that 3-5 traits aren't sufficient, but a list of 20 is probably overwhelming and impractical. For some reason, 12 seemed to be about right. And besides, there's something that feels complete about the number 12. Eggs are sold in dozens, and donuts, also (even though the term "baker's dozen" actually means 13.... There's no way we're going to jinx ourselves and pick thirteen!), and there are also 12 months in a year and 12 years in the life of a student from elementary to high school in the U.S. So, without much more scientific reasoning than that, here are the twelve essential qualities of successful students that we've chosen to discuss in this book.

We believe that successful students....

1. Discover their purpose
2. Learn how to learn
3. Think critically
4. Value effort more than intellect
5. Embrace failure
6. Build relationships
7. Ask for help
8. Help others
9. Manage time
10. Invest in their health
11. Manage money
12. Harness technology

For each of these qualities, we'll share stories of students who are not quite college ready, observations from our experience as higher education professionals, and advice that can help you, as a parent, equip and strengthen your student for success now and in college. As faculty and administrators, we have purposely chosen to present a viewpoint from a college perspective to share with parents of high school students who aspire to attend college.

We recognize that the college environment can be a mysterious and daunting place, inhabited by lots of people with Ph.D.'s who may seem a bit unapproachable and intimidating. We want to lift that veil for parents and help them recognize and develop the traits that will help their students be successful in the college environment as well as strategies for strengthening those traits before college begins.

What This Book Is *Not*

We are parents of high-school aged students who are, themselves, preparing for the college experience, *but* we don't intend for this to be a book about parenting, per se. While we are dedicated parents, we certainly don't feel like experts, and there are already scores of books and advice available on parenting strategies, techniques, and philosophies. Instead, our focus is on how parents can help students prepare to be successful in college, based on what we *do* know from our years of experience in higher education.

What If You're Not a Parent?

We titled this book *A High School Parent's Guide to College Success: 12 Essentials* and have chosen to use the word "parent" throughout the book, but in doing so, we recognize that there are many adults who find themselves caring for high-school-aged students, including foster parents, neighbors, grandparents, aunts, uncles, and other relatives. We designed this book to be helpful for *any adult* who is in a position to care for and influence a young person with college aspirations. We use the term "parent" to simplify our writing, but we want our readers to know that everything we include in this book is intended to be relevant for the broad, inclusive definition we offer here.

How to Use This Book

You can read this book in the order we've presented the essential qualities, or you can skip around as your interests guide you. We don't want to claim that there's anything magical about the order in which we've presented these 12 essential qualities, and there's no requirement that you read the first chapter before reading the second chapter. We expect that different qualities will resonate with different parents differently, based on their own perspectives and what they know to be true about their students. We encourage skimming (There will *not* be a quiz at the end of class!) to find what resonates with you, and we hope that you'll experience this book as a family and not just individually.

To that end, each chapter includes the following:

- From High School to College Stories. These are common stories of students who are transitioning from high school to college and the issues they face. Although they are presented as to illustrate the transition from high school to college, we provide information following each story that could help them develop college-readiness skills.
- Parent Tips. Placed throughout each chapter are parent tips for helping your student become college ready.
- Parent-Student Conversation Starters. Each chapter provides questions or prompts for talking with your student. Consider the questions as suggestions for getting your student to think—and possibly act—on the ideas in the chapter.
- Parent Resources. At the end of each chapter, we provide a short list of recommended readings and resources. We include a brief summary and the reasons we feel the resource is worth your time.

We expect some parents to wonder if we recommend this book for students. We certainly think the content is suitable for them, and it can be helpful, but we wrote it primarily for parents. Nonetheless, we offer a number of suggestions about how to stimulate conversations with your student around certain qualities, and those conversations do not require your student to have read the book. If your student is in his junior or senior year in high school and is dealing with AP classes, SAT and ACT tests, club and sports activities, and a blooming social life, we acknowledge the reality that he may be unlikely or unwilling to devote time to reading this with the same vigor as you might. Thus, we leave it to you to decide whether to encourage your student to read this book, too. Above all, we want this book to be for parents, like us, who have worked hard for 20 years or more raising a child, toddler, adolescent, teen, and young adult, hoping to help him become the person they know he can become. The depth of love we have, as parents, for our kids is staggering, and it can be a harrowing experience to prepare to let them go, so to speak, off to a college experience and a larger world beyond those four years. We hope this book provides helpful guidance and reassurance to you. As lifelong educators who work with college students every day, thank you for all you do to prepare the next generation for success.

A Special Note about Pronouns

In each chapter, we will use a singular pronoun to refer to "your student" to keep our editor happy (and our 8th grade English teacher happy as well. Hello, Mrs. Lamberth-Neeley! We know you are reading this with a red pen in hand!). To keep it easy on the reader—and the authors—the gender of the pronoun will reflect the gender of the student in the From High School to College story. Occasionally, we will talk about "our students," and then, of course, will use the appropriate pronoun.

Part I
Academics and Learning

Chapter 1
Successful students discover their purpose.

How many young people know what their purpose is? For that matter, how many adults have a strong sense of purpose? We know many people who determined early in their lives what they wanted to do or become, and we also know people who are well past middle age and are still figuring that out. Nonetheless, we are willing to bet that if you picked up this book, you feel on some level that your student has not quite figured that out yet or has a few possibilities, but she is not sure which direction to go.

Developing a sense of purpose does not mean that your student must have it "all figured out" by the time she graduates from high school, but it does mean that your student should begin the exploration of what potential paths interest her and what she may want to explore now to prepare her for life after high school and even a potential college major. To that end, this chapter helps you prepare your student for the conversations and contemplations that will help her figure out what her purpose is or at least which path she wants to take to develop a sense of purpose.

From High School to College Story: Madison

Madison started high school nervous about moving to a different school. She went from a small, private religious-based middle school to a large public high school where she didn't know anyone. She had difficulty adjusting and never felt as though she fit in despite developing friendships with several classmates. The thought of going to college made her even more anxious because she had heard how hard it was to make friends there as well. Graduating from high school and deciding what to do next felt paralyzing, so she decided to not think about it. Instead, she spent a lot of time hiking on local trails. She liked the solitude and the quiet—no one constantly asking her how things are going. She felt she could hike all day, every day, but knew that no one would think that was a good long-term plan: hiking for a living, if that was even possible.

Her strategy seemed to work until the beginning of her last semester in high school. Colleges were sending her information about upcoming deadlines to apply, her parents were asking her what she planned to do after graduation, and her high school counselor tried to show her what other options, if not college, were available to her. She had not really participated in many activities during high school except for a church sewing group. She helped make dresses for underprivileged children in South America and often spent time creating her own outfits to wear. Both hiking and sewing were hobbies she could do by herself when she wanted and with others when she wanted, but usually she chose to do them alone.

As far as academics, she was in the middle of her class— neither a high-achieving student nor a failing student— which meant that she got lost in the shuffle. When her English teacher asked her to write about her future plans, she confided in her teacher that she really didn't have any plans and didn't know what to do about it.

Madison did not feel college ready. In fact, she did not feel ready for anything.

Helping Your Student Explore a Purpose

Madison's story represents those high school students who sincerely answer the question "What are you going to do after high school" with "I don't know" as well as those students who seem to lack motivation or lack someone else (like a parent or coach) driving the process. A high school student who does not have even a spark of an idea of where to go—even *if* she wants to go to college—and what to study is not unusual. In fact, it is perfectly normal, and we are not advocating that your high school student has it all figured out by the end of 9th grade. Instead, we recognize that this is an opportunity for finding out who your student will become. We encourage you and your student to begin the exploration process by observing and recording what she likes to do now.

Here are some actions you can take now to help her figure out what she wants to do or could do after high school:

#1 Make a list of what your student already does. Does your student participate in certain volunteer groups, religious organizations, athletics, fine and performing arts, or community projects? There are hints in the kinds of activities students participate in and the kinds of people they surround themselves with as to what they like to do and what they may do in the future.

Take for instance, one of the authors. Amy participated in the following activities in high school: speech and writing contests, theatre, tutoring, taking and teaching art, teaching swimming lessons, lifeguarding, babysitting, swimming, running, and reading for pleasure. These activities were mostly ones that she chose because she liked them and some were chosen because she had friends who did them (the athletic endeavors were chosen in this manner). Notice that at least one common thread in these activities is performing and another common thread is teaching; of course, there is also the thread of creating (art, speeches, and writing). It should be no surprise that she continued (except for the athletic activities) these interests into college and participates in them now almost every day as a professor, author, and speaker. Had someone told her 16-year-old self that what she was doing then would be part of what she would be doing for a living, she thinks she would have dismissed it, in part because she didn't see the connection between what she liked to do early in her life and what she would be doing as an adult.

> **Parent Tip:** Routinely ask what your student is learning or doing and what she likes about the experiences.

#2 Make a list of what your student is interested in doing, but hasn't done yet. What does she want to do that she hasn't done yet because of age, skill, or opportunity? Asking a teenager "What is your dream in life?" or "What is your life's purpose?" may be a quick road to silence or may elicit the usual "I don't know" response, but the question "What kinds of experiences are you interested in that you have not done yet?" is less threatening and can serve as a way of exploring general likes and dislikes.

Madison, for example, was interested in hiking and learning how to make her own clothes. While these are two very different activities, investigating them both may yield some valuable information about her that she can use to continue to determine her options after she graduates from high school. Both activities can be solitary or at least do not depend on lots of other people to accomplish. One activity revolves around nature and movement (i.e., the movement of walking from one place to another) and the other revolves around creativity and producing something tangible (i.e., a piece of clothing). This information may give Madison some ideas about what seems to occupy her interests and what she would like to explore in college. At least for now, she seems drawn to interacting with the outdoors and creating items for her own personal consumption. If Madison is more aware of her interests, she will be more likely to match those interests to opportunities and even programs of study when she gets to college.

> **Parent Tip:** Instead of asking, "What do you want to do with the rest of your life?" ask "What would you like to do if only for a little while?"

#3 Make a list of what your student can do for hours on end. In the 1970s, positive psychologist Mihaly Csikszentmihalyi studied the concept known as "flow," or the act of being involved in an activity and feeling so engaged that one loses track of time.[1] Your student may find it difficult to think of one thing that she has done with this kind of enthusiasm and focus, but we bet she could describe what activities would fill a "perfect day" or what activities she most enjoys. Video games and sports often top such a list of for high school students, so be prepared to hear similar answers. This does not mean you must encourage your student to major in computer programming or sports medicine. Recording these activities is just part of the process of raising self-awareness.

#4 Consider different options for your student after high school. Even though the heart of this book is getting you and your student ready for college, it is worth talking through different pathways for life after high school. Not every student steps off the graduation stage onto a college campus three months later, nor should every student follow that path if it is not the right next step for her. Spend some time talking about what she *thinks* she may be interested in (see the lists that you made from the previous questions) and determine which ones have a direct line to college or another institution of higher education. Consider the following questions as you explore these potential alternative pathways:

- Do your student's interests require a college degree or certification for making a living?
- Can your student explore her interests in other ways than sitting in a classroom?
- What kinds of college experiences and degrees would align with your student's interests?
- What kind of "real world" experience would deepen your student's interests?

#5 Determine what else your student needs to do. Are there any other experiences or activities that would help your student develop a sense of purpose or direction in life? An opportunity to shadow a professional or to work (even briefly) in a field that interests your student could give her information about what she likes and what she does not. Keep in mind, though, that such experiences should not close doors permanently—anyone could have an unpleasant experience exploring her interests. Other ways to get your student thinking about a purpose is to do one or more of the following:

- Ask friends, family, and acquaintances how they discovered what they like to do, what jobs/careers they have had, and what they wished they had done differently when they were in high school.
- Look for classes, volunteer opportunities, and other experiences that could provide insight into likes and dislikes. A cooking class, a community park clean-up day, or a face-painting booth at a festival are all rich experiences that can provide opportunities to explore.
- Read blogs and books, listen to podcasts and audiobooks, and watch videos of interesting topics.

Start the conversation with these suggestions, but don't assume that your student will resolve her uncertainties with one talk. You can be assured, though, that the questions you ask and the discovery process you participate in will help your student consider the possibilities. Be patient with the process. We see students enter college with the same qualms about making important decisions, but they eventually take a course or complete a project that sparks their curiosity and leads them down the path to making a decision about college, career, or a life.

> **Parent Tip:** Make a list of your student's strengths and positive qualities and review that list with her.

Finding Meaning in Past Experiences

Let's revisit Madison's story. We know what she does as hobbies, but we don't know what else her experiences may tell her about her purpose. When we counsel students to develop their sense of purpose (usually when we work with them to choose a college major), we help them switch their thinking from the future (*What do I want to be or do?*) to the past (*What did I enjoy doing before I came to college? What do those experiences tell me about myself?*). Thinking about the past is often more accessible for students—they lived it, right?—and less likely to cause them the "analysis paralysis" we see when they are faced with so many choices. Katharine Brooks, in her book *You Majored in What?: Mapping Your Path from Chaos to Career*, suggests a process for figuring out a pathway that begins with listing significant moments, awards, recognitions, jobs, and even praise. Here is a list of questions that you can ask to start the conversation:[2]

- What awards or honors has your student earned?
- What classes does your student show the most interest in?
- What kinds of people does your student like? Whom does she admire? Why?

- What significant experiences has your student had?
- What accomplishment is your student most proud of?
- What quality, trait, or action has your student been complimented for?
- What jobs has your student had? What work has your student done (paid or not paid)?

Another approach to figuring out how the past may shed light on your student's future is to ask her to record what she said she wanted to be when she grew up at different points in her life. Then, ask her what influenced that idea. For example, Madison wanted to be a ballerina when she was five years old. What influenced that decision was an older cousin who wore beautiful recital costumes. Madison loved playing dress up in her cousin's leotards and tutus. This information can serve as a clue to help Madison figure out her own pathways.

> **Parent Tip:** Look for opportunities to praise your student for developing a difficult skill or trying something new.

When you have completed a list of past experiences, the next step according to Katharine Brooks, is to look for connections or themes. Does your student always seem to be asked for advice? Has your student been praised for leading others or organizing help for someone in need? Those connections and themes serve as a conversation starter as to what your student may want to continue to do for a living.

Making a Difference in Others' Lives

In the college classes that we teach, we often use a well-known activity called "The 5 Whys."[3] We start our students with the first question: "Why are you in college?" Each answer then helps to form the next "Why?" For example, if a student answers the question "Why are you in college?" with "I want to earn a degree in accounting," we then ask, "Why do you want to earn a degree in accounting?" The activity concludes after five questions that start with "why" are asked and answered. At the end of the activity, many students declare that the reason "why" is to help others. Angela Duckworth, in her research on grit, argues that a person who sees her life's purpose as benefitting others in need is a person who is more likely to demonstrate resilience and be successful.[4] So, it is worth asking your student if she wants to help others as part of the process of discovering a purpose. To help your student consider how she can benefit others, here are just a few questions that you can ask:

- What world, national, or community problems interest you?
- If you could solve one problem, what would it be?
- If you could help only a small group of people, who would it be?
- What problems do you *not* want to solve?
- What types of people would you *not* be interested in helping?

As with the answers to all the conversation starters we offer in this chapter, consider them to be the beginning of the conversation and exploration about purpose. If your student feels confident that she knows what her life's purpose is, then walking through these questions can help her feel more confident she is on the right path or it may offer her additional ways to fulfill her purpose.

> **Parent Tip:** Ask your student how she would want to make a difference in the world or what problem she would want to work on.

Let's go back once more to Madison's story. By answering the questions above, she realized that she was often praised by classmates on her clothing choices and her style. She also remembered the fun she had playing dress up with her cousin's costumes. While she wanted to be a ballerina when she was younger, she reflected on what influenced her to make that decision and recognized it was not the physical activity of dance that interested her, but the outfits that ballerinas wear that caught her attention. This insight can help her explore this potential pathway to determine what her purpose could be. Designing and making clothes is a fun activity and could be a career, but helping others look their best and feel their best in their clothes is a purpose that can fulfill Madison for a long time.

Your student may be in a similar situation as Madison, but rest assured that she can start the process of developing a sense of purpose—or at least developing an awareness of what that purpose could be—with some intentional reflections on what she likes to do, what she has done already, and what she may want to do in the future.

From High School to College Conversation Starters

Use these questions to get the conversation going with your student. Revisit them regularly throughout your student's high school and early college career:

- What have been your favorite classes in school so far and why?
- What skill(s) or trait(s) has someone complimented you for?
- What do you want to do but have not done yet because of time, money, or experience?
- If you knew you would not fail, what would you do?

Parent Resources

Brooks, Katharine. *You Majored in What?: Mapping Your Path from Chaos to Career*. Plume, 2010.

If you have a student about to go to college, you need to read this book together. You will have less anxiety about what she decides to major in and more tools to help her (and you, if you need it) find the major or career that most aligns with her interests and passions. Brooks combines insights about college majors and the needs of the workplace with creative, energizing activities.

WHY WE LOVE IT: It is the first book that we have found that provides a realistic path for balancing your student's interests with a path to a college major and a career; however, it is also a great read for a high school student as she starts to think about what interests her and what she has already experienced.

~~~

Bruni, Frank. *Where You Go Is Not Who'll You Be: An Antidote to the College Admissions Mania.* Grand Central Publishing, 2016.

If you are caught up in the frenzy of talking about where your student is going to college and either judging others or feeling judged, this book is for you. While it may not alleviate all your fears about helping your future college student choose the best college, it will provide you with many reasons why you can relax with the knowledge that where your student goes is not the end of the story. It matters more, according to the author, what your student does while in college. Bruni delves into the alma maters of top CEOs and award winners to see what, if any, connection exists between success and name-brand, ivy-covered institutions. The conclusion: State schools and affordable alternatives appear as often or even more so on the lists of successful people.

WHY WE LOVE IT: It is the perfect antidote to super-competitive parents who are fixated on sending their student to the "best" college. It also provides a real look at who gets into those coveted schools and why. Finally, it gives concrete steps for helping your future college student make the most out of her own experience.

~~~

Damon, William. *The Path to Purpose: How Young People Find Their Calling in Life.* Free Press, 2009.

William Damon has spent his life studying adolescents, so he knows a thing or two about the process of moving through childhood into adulthood. This book provides a comprehensive discussion about how teenagers develop a sense of purpose and what we can do to help nurture it.

WHY WE LOVE IT: This book provides research-based reasons for why teenagers must go through the process of finding their purpose so they won't experience "failure to launch" and find themselves living in our basements.

Chapter 2
Successful students learn how to learn.

How do you best learn a skill or topic of knowledge? By reading about it? Listening to someone else explain it? Watching someone demonstrate it? By trying it yourself? Different readers of this book will answer this question differently, and that leads to the central point of this chapter—learning is an individualized, personal experience. Your student, then, needs to understand for himself how he learns and the habits he needs to develop and maintain to learn effectively.

Why is it important for your student develop strong learning habits when he obviously demonstrated learning from kindergarten to high school? The answer in part is because the nature of learning in college may differ greatly. For sure, the learning will be more intense and focused and there will be an expectation that your student to learn the material outside of his classes and most likely without the intervention of the professors. This chapter underscores the importance of knowing how to learn as a method for getting your student ready for the learning that will be required after high school.

From High School to College Story: Max

Max had known about his Attention Deficit Hyperactivity Disorder (ADHD) for as long as he can remember, and while he didn't completely understand it, he realized that it's part of who he is and it influenced how he lived his life including how he performed in school. What seemed easy to his classmates—sitting still, listening, taking notes, focusing—felt impossible to him. And yet, somehow, with the help of his parents, tutors, teachers, and friends, and mostly because of a lot of extra hard work and practice, he managed to perform well enough in high school to get on the path to college.

While the idea of having greater freedom and independence in college is exciting, Max also recognized that the college experience would present an entirely new set of challenges for him. In high school, his parents managed schedules and incorporated support systems to help him succeed academically even though his ADHD made it more difficult for him to focus on tasks and complete them without being distracted or sidetracked. Both he and his parents have realized, however, that they won't be there with him to maintain the same level of control and restraint. On some days, Max feels excited about the prospect of freedom and independence in college, but on other days, he struggles with a sense of dread and panic. What if he can't learn what he needs to in college because of his ADHD?

> **Parent Tip:** Read and discuss the recommended resources we list at the end of this chapter. The book *Make It Stick*, for example, is available both in hardcopy and as an audio book.

Learning How We Learn

Your student may not have ADHD like Max, but Max's story is still relevant because it illustrates the importance of knowing how we learn and how to develop habits and practices in college that support and facilitate learning. For Max and others with ADHD, effective learning may require extra measures to reduce distractions while studying or taking tests: flash cards to aid memorization and strategies that link one piece of information to another to strengthen how deeply and strongly a particular concept is held in memory for the long term. For others, effective learning might be aided through participation in group study teams or by seeking tutoring support.

In general, here are three important points about the concept of learning, particularly in the context of high school students transitioning to college:

#1 The learning and studying habits that worked in high school may not work well in college. This is because the sheer quantity of information that students are expected to process in college is much larger, and the depth of understanding and analysis that students are supposed to achieve is higher as well.

#2 High school students who have been rewarded for finding the path of least resistance and least effort in high school will naturally face greater challenges in college. Some of the most impressive students in high school by virtue of their GPA's and test scores are often the most vulnerable to significant academic setbacks during their first year because they don't expect to fail or have difficulty with new challenges, and thus, are the least prepared for it when it happens. Even for valedictorians, B's and C's happen in college, and these good-but-less-than-perfect grades are a normal and predictable experience in college.

#3 Learning is principally about memory, and there are no easy paths or shortcuts to achieve the level of

memorization that's necessary for deep learning to occur. The paradox that we've seen with college students is that those who have struggled with learning in high school and had to adapt through a lot of extra effort, hard work, and learning strategies are actually better positioned for success in college, particularly in their first year, than students who experienced relatively effortless success in high school. The latter students haven't yet developed studying and learning habits that foster memorization, interconnected topics, memory retrieval, and other effective learning strategies because, to this point in their lives, they haven't needed to. They also haven't experienced failure, so they are more susceptible to being devastated and discouraged when they receive less-than-perfect grades in college.

> **Parent Tip:** Encourage your student to pursue challenging learning situations. For high-achieving high school students, it may be helpful for them to take a few college classes at a local community college or university to experience college-level instruction and coursework.

Creating a Learning Environment and Learning Strategies

So, how can you, as a parent, help your student develop effective learning habits as he prepares for college? Effective learning is, in some ways, like a bountiful garden—it requires the right conditions and the right activities to occur. For your student to become an effective learner in college means that he needs to create the right environment to support his learning and to engage in the right activities to foster that learning.

An effective learning environment for your student might include the following:

- In high school, a study space in his room that includes a desk, laptop computer with reliable Internet access, calculator, writing materials and noise-cancelling headphones to help him concentrate.
- In college, study spaces across campus that are designed with learning and studying in mind, like the library, student union, or buildings that house classrooms. These spaces can serve as alternatives to his room when it's not convenient or possible to study there, or when he needs to add a bit of variety to his study schedule.

Once the right learning environment has been established and identified, the next step is to develop and practice effective learning strategies that are tailored to both the topic of study and how your student learns best. These strategies might include the following:

#1 Flash cards. Creating flash cards is particularly useful for reviewing and memorizing content and can be used by the student himself or in group study situations. Online flash card programs such as Quizlet are popular and effective, too.

#2 Practice quizzes and tests. Professors sometimes provide students with access to practice exams and quizzes to help students recall important information and prepare for the types of questions they will encounter in graded activities. It's always a good idea to use those practice materials when professors offer them.

#3 Interspersing topics and material with each other. Research has shown that when topics and information are linked to each other in some way, people learn them more deeply. Students are sometimes tempted to focus on only one topic at a time, with the thinking that they'll learn Topic A first, then Topic B, and so on. But it's often more effective to study and learn Topic A for a certain period of time, and then jump to Topic B for some time, and then back to Topic A, while looking for and considering whether there are connections between those topics. For example, the topic of supply and demand in economics is closely related to what economics call equilibrium pricing, so it's helpful to take time to consider how those two concepts relate to one another. Instead of just focusing on supply and demand before studying pricing, it's a better idea to read and learn about supply and demand, and then move on to pricing, and then back again, looking for connections and interrelationships. This type of strategy will actually help your student learn both topics more deeply.

#4 Studying with others. Group study sessions, managed properly, can complement the time that students spend learning on their own. By joining a study group of motivated students, your student can calibrate and test his own learning against others. It's also helpful to have one student test or quiz another student on a topic by simulating the types of questions anticipated on future quizzes and exams. Finally, the group dynamic can have a motivating and encouraging impact on students who find themselves tired, discouraged, or confused when studying alone. It's important to note that group study is not a substitute for individual study, but a complement, so your student still needs to devote time to studying content on his own.

#5 Spreading the learning over time. One of the primary reasons why professors and tutors discourage students from "cramming" for exams the night before the test is because this practice does not facilitate effective learning. The most effective way to deeply learn a subject is to spread that learning over time and intersperse learning on one topic with another. For example, if a student is taking classes in chemistry, math, and English composition during a particular term, it would be more effective if the student studied each topic for bursts of time during the term and alternated between the classes, rather than trying to focus only on one topic or class for long durations as described above.

Let's revisit Max's story and his learning challenges. First, he is fortunate to have parents who are aware of how to build on his learning strengths and interests since his diagnosis. Also, he has been used to modifying learning strategies to fit his needs, so making the step from high school learning to college learning will be a little easier. Max will still need to work hard and make changes to his learning habits as needed, ask for help, and check with his professors about his progress. All of these tasks are what students who are developing college-ready habits needs to be doing, and the more you can cultivate those habits with your student while he is in high school, the smoother that transition will be when he begins college.

> **Parent Tip:** Connect your student with successful college students. This will provide a great peer-to-peer connection for your student to hear, firsthand, about the adjustments they had to make in college and how they learned about their own learning.

Parent-Student Conversation Starters

Use these questions to get the conversation going with your student. Revisit them regularly throughout your student's high school and early college career:

- How did you learn how to [insert a skill here] or how did you learn so much about [insert an area of knowledge here]? Encourage your student to go back in time to consider how he learned to tie his own shoes, ride a bike, drive a car, play a musical instrument, write a sentence, or solve a math problem. What were the challenges and obstacles along the way, and what strategies did your student employ to overcome them? It will be both informational and inspirational for your student to reflect on everything he has already learned, and how he did it, to help him develop a plan to do so in college.
- What does it mean to learn something?
- How do you learn best? What does that look like for you? What will that look like in college?
- What will be different in college that will require different strategies for your learning? This is a particularly useful conversation to have when you are visiting college campuses. If possible, visit a college campus while school is in session,

and observe students studying in the library, meeting as groups, and engaged in other learning-related activities. Then talk with your student about his own strategies. Ask your student "Where will you study in college? When? How? With whom? What will be the barriers and distractions to learning in the college environment, and how can you overcome them?

Parent Resources

Sanders, Matthew L. *Becoming a Learner: Realizing the Opportunity of Education.* Institute for Communication & Leadership, 2012.

This book really helps to answer the "why?" question about a college education and focuses the reader on how learning helps you become a better person—a learner—rather than just emphasizing the practical benefits of a college education towards a career. It's not a long book, so you and your student can tackle it without a major investment of time. It has chapter titles like "Principles of Learning" that offering universally-useful principles like "learning can't be cheated" that provide enduring truths to guide your student as a lifelong learner.

WHY WE LOVE IT: It's a concise, inspirational book that will get you and your student excited about learning and see it as an opportunity, not something to be endured or tolerated. It will also serve as an encouragement to those who struggle in their learning due to cognitive or behavioral challenges or other difficulties.

~~~

Brown, Peter C., Roediger, Henry L. III, and McDaniel, Mark A. *Make It Stick*. The Belknap Press, 2014.

As parents (and teachers) we're prone to say things like "study hard!" to our students in an attempt to offer helpful advice in their efforts to learn effectively and perform well in their classes. *Make It Stick* is a compilation of the latest research on learning theory that provides practical and counterintuitive advice about how to learn most effectively. One piece of advice for parents when reading this—first try to apply the principles from the book to your own learning before offering suggestions to your student about his own learning.

WHY WE LOVE IT: This book provides research and science-based suggestions that are practical and accessible to everyone who wants to become a better learner. Perhaps the biggest takeaway is that we tend to be learning the most when that learning feels the hardest.

~~~

Hallowell, Edward M. and Ratey, John J. *Delivered from Distraction: Getting the Most out of Life with Attention Deficit Disorder*. Ballantine Books, 2005.

There are a lot of books in the marketplace about ADD and ADHD, but we've chosen to recommend this one because of the research and expertise on which it is based and because it has a chapter titled "Major Danger Alert: College and ADD" that offers a lot of practical and valuable advice for parents to effectively prepare their students for college. The authors provide ten specific steps that parents can take, starting during the senior year in high school, to help their students prepare for the college experience. These steps are useful and practical for any students, not just those with ADD.

WHY WE LOVE IT: This book helps parents and others better understand ADD and appreciate it from a strengths-based perspective, rather than as a sickness or disease. The practical advice about preparing a student for college makes the book particularly valuable for parents of high school students.

Chapter 3
Successful students know that effort matters more than intellect.

Emphasizing effort over talent or intellect has gained some momentum in K-12 and higher education over the past decade, and we as educators and parents are glad to see this shift. It gives students more ownership over the learning process and helps students more appropriately frame setbacks and failures.

Students who can regularly embrace the mindset that they can improve any skill through deliberate practice, feedback, and adjustment are more likely to be successful not just in college, but also in anything they attempt to master. Parents can play a significant role in helping students change their thinking from "I'm not good at this" (whether "this" is math, writing, or test-taking) to "I'm not good at this...yet...but I can be." This chapter focuses on how and why effort is such an important part of the learning process and provides you with suggestions for helping your student put more effort into his tasks.

From High School to College Story: Casey

Casey learned to play the saxophone when he was 7 years old. By the time he reached high school and played in the jazz and marching bands, he was called "talented" and "a prodigy" by those who attended his concerts, but they didn't know how much time he spent practicing. He loved the compliments. In fact, he had spent countless hours for more than a decade practicing and performing. His dedication to the saxophone paid off when he received a full scholarship to an out-of-state university that is known for its highly competitive musical performance program. When he left for college, he had the chops of a professional musician, but he realized that first he wanted to complete a degree.

Casey's first semester of college was filled with music and general education courses. As a condition of his scholarship, he had to participate in 10 hours of practice a week. He also decided to join a fraternity. He had put so much time and effort into playing the saxophone over the past 11 years and was such a skilled musician that he didn't think he needed to work as hard any more. There were other things he wanted to participate in and music would just be a part of his week, but not the dominant activity.

Despite his busy weekly schedule, he earned passing grades by mid-term and felt confident that he could raise some of his grades to meet the requirements of his music scholarship. It wasn't until the last few weeks of the term that his grades started plummeting and it looked as though he would not end the semester with the 3.25 GPA that his scholarship required. He had A's in his music classes, but D's and F's in his general education classes. He wasn't too worried because he knew he could retake any classes he failed; besides, he was succeeding in the classes that mattered the most to him and to his degree.

The next semester he maintained the same schedule and re-enrolled in the classes he failed. While his GPA was well below a 3.25, he had another semester to make up for his low grades the previous semester. He reasoned that the worst-case scenario would be that he would have to pay for college through loans should he lose his scholarship. Casey soon realized that his music classes were more demanding and because he was not spending enough time practicing, he was having trouble mastering the more challenging pieces he was required to learn. The harsh, but honest feedback from his professors confirmed to him that he was not performing well. While his professors emphasized the need to spend more time and focus on working through difficult arrangements, Casey started to wonder if he was not as talented as he had originally thought he was. Maybe majoring in music and dreaming of being a famous performer were out of his reach.

Casey limped along throughout his second semester and ended his first year in college by losing his music scholarship and landing on probation for a 1.75 GPA. He was convinced that he did not have what it takes to master the well-known program's high expectations— they just seemed more challenging than what he experienced in high school. He also knew he needed to make some major changes over the summer to improve his GPA and get back on track with a degree. He had a lot to think about for the next few months.

Is It Better to Work Hard or Be Talented?

Casey's situation is not an uncommon story for high-achieving high school students. You can easily replace Casey's accomplishments in music with anything else that high school students dedicate themselves to as adolescents. They may have spent countless hours perfecting a skill and have been fortunate to have the support from family, teachers, coaches, and trainers. The demanding work that they spent getting into a specific program or earning a top scholarship for their achievement may seem as though it was not enough to maintain their status as a top talent if with those accolades comes the expectation to achieve even higher levels of success. They have gotten "in," but can they stay there? Self-doubt starts to creep in, too, as they are now surrounded by many other students who have dedicated just as much time and effort to perfecting their craft as well. This can be particularly stressful if they were the "best" at their school or in their community.

Carol Dweck's best-selling book *Mindset: The New Psychology of Success* makes the case that people have either a fixed mindset or a growth mindset.[5] A person with a fixed mindset believes that intelligence is fixed, or unchangeable. That person also believes that setbacks and challenges are indications that they are not "good at" the task. A person with a growth mindset, on the other hand, believes improvement in any skill comes from sustained effort that uses setbacks, challenges, and feedback as opportunities to get better.

Casey demonstrated a growth mindset before he got to college—he practiced, which often included correcting mistakes, and he used feedback from his music teachers to become a skilled musician. However, once he got to college, the challenge increased—as did his desire to do other things—and he did not adjust for those changes. Instead, he found the comparison to his fellow musicians and the criticism from his professors discouraging. Did Casey reach a peak of learning that he cannot rise above? Not according to Dweck, who would say that

Casey embraced a fixed mindset when faced with these new challenges. His first step would be to recognize that more effort is needed to reach the next level of mastery.

As the Brain "Grows"

What could help Casey is a reminder of how he became a celebrated saxophone player in the first place: Simply put, he worked for it. He spent countless hours for over a decade practicing, deliberately as we will describe later, and perfecting his craft by challenging himself and learning from his mistakes. Despite what others may have said to praise him, Casey was not *born playing the saxophone*, but he was, according to the research of Dr. Rita Smilkstein, *born to learn* how to master a musical instrument. Smilkstein's aptly named book *We're Born to Learn* describes how the brain, specifically the "dendrites" in the brain, reacts when we learn how to do something.[6] She notes that through *effort* we "grow," or create longer, more intricately connected dendrites in our brain.

Think of the dendrites as roads between locations you want to go. The more pavement that is put down and the wider the road, the easier it is to get from one location to the other. This is a similar process when someone is learning something new. The better the "roads" to the information, knowledge, or skill, the easier it is to access that information, knowledge, or skill. Highly practiced musicians, as Casey was in his early years, can easily access that skill because the neural pathways are well established. If the roads are not well traveled—think about a skill you used to have but stopped practicing or using—they may become overgrown and hard to navigate through at first. The same is true of your dendrites: If you don't use the neural pathway, it may get "overgrown" and difficult to access at least initially. This doesn't mean you can never get to that location again; you just may need to clear that path through some extra practice.

> **Parent Tip:** Consider how you talk about others' successes and failures. Do you attribute others' success to talent or hard work? Do you demonstrate a lack of appreciation (and subsequently a negative view of) mistakes that people make? Your student will reflect your viewpoint of both success and failure, at least early in his development.

Practice Makes...Learning?

Angela Duckworth, who is known for her research on grit and her 2013 TED Talk, which has been viewed almost 10 million times, writes about the function of *deliberate practice* in her book *Grit: The Power and Passion of Perseverance* on the subject. People who exhibit grit, or the ability to stick to a task despite challenges, can do so because they have put sustained, focused effort into getting better at a skill.[7] That practiced skill makes it easier to persevere when the going gets tough. Duckworth emphasizes the secret to "practice makes perfect": The practice needs to be deliberately challenging and focused.[8]

To illustrate this point, consider the descriptions of two people who go to the gym for a total of 10 hours a week. The first person goes to the gym with no goal or plan, but instead moves from treadmill to weight machine as he feels like it. He doesn't keep track of his time or effort at each machine and barely breaks a sweat. The second person has a specific goal—increased strength and muscle tone—and goes with a plan for what machines to use, how much weight to lift, how many reps to do, and how much rest to take between sets. Same amount of time spent per week, but the second person's deliberate practice and plan for making improvements to her strength and muscle tone can be measured in her results. The first person can only say he spends time at a gym, but it is not likely he will become more fit. It's a physiological fact that you cannot increase your strength and muscle mass if you don't increase the weight you lift or increase the frequency and intensity over time. It is how you build muscle, and it is how you get better at anything: You do it through working on that muscle or skill repeatedly over time and participating in more challenging activities with each practice.

Parent Tip: Learn and model a growth mindset yourself. Is there a hobby or skill you've always wanted to develop, but haven't? It's one thing to tell your student with words about working hard and sticking to something even when failure occurs, but it's far more powerful to demonstrate a growth mindset by committing time and effort to a new learning challenge before his very eyes.

It's What You Say, Not Just How You Say It

Another key component of using effort to make improvements is feedback. As a musician in high school,

Casey used feedback from his performances to determine what he needed to work on. It is hard to ignore a wrong note when you hear it! Casey also received advice on how to get better from his music teachers. The process of feedback did not change from high school to college, but the nature of the feedback may have, as did the expectations he had to meet.

In addition to her work on mindset, Carol Dweck has written about the power of the word "yet" when giving feedback.[9] The word "yet" underscores the growth mindset in that it conveys a sense that more work is needed and improvement is achievable. Consider these two statements: "Your thesis is not clear" and "Your thesis is not clear yet." For some students, the first statement seems final, unchangeable. Those same students may feel that additional work is not needed or required. The second statement that includes "yet" conveys a different message. It implies that more work is needed, but that the thesis can become clear. There is hope and an expectation to make a change.

As a parent, you are in an advantageous position to provide feedback that promotes the growth mindset. When your student stumbles, falls short of desired achievement, or even fails, what you say is just as important as how you say it: Remind your student that with effort and deliberate, focused work, he can improve. How you refer to mistakes and failures, too, can set your student up for additional success. Mistakes, like wrong notes, happen and are part of the process of learning and doing better next time.

> **Parent Tip:** Adopt the language of growth mindset in your discussions. The Mindset Works® website offers several examples of how parents can change their verbal encouragements and feedback to better instill and reinforce a growth mindset in their students.
> https://www.mindsetworks.com/parents/growth-mindset-parenting

Cultivating "Stick-to-itiveness"

We really wish there was a better word to describe staying focused and committed to a task over an extended period other than "stick-to-itiveness." For sure, the words *persistence*, *perseverance*, and *tenacity* come close, but they don't create the visual image that "stick-to-itiveness" does. So far, in this chapter we have talked about growing dendrites, participating in deliberate practice, and providing helpful feedback. All of these activities take effort, so it is not surprising that sticking to a task or activity is also part of this chapter because when the going gets tough, it takes effort to hang in there and continue. According to Angela Duckworth, sustained effort over time is an indicator of a gritty person.[10] What this means is that a person who works through the hard times of a task or an activity, such as a particularly difficult course or a challenging sport, is building long-term skills of resilience, or the ability to bounce back from adversity.

Let's go back to Casey's story and figure out where he may have gotten off track. It should be noted that he may have decided that he wants to try other things and not focus on performing arts as a major or career path. Another possibility is that he was caught off guard by the increase in distractions and performance expectations. If he is only facing a temporary setback, he can remind himself that he has already proven for more than a decade that focused effort and practice build skills. He can also remind himself that his failing, or suffering setbacks, is part of the process of mastering a skill and strengthen resolve. While he has been placed on probation for his grades, he still can make changes and most likely spend considerable more effort and time on his classes.

Parent-Student Conversation Starters

Use these questions to get the conversation going with your student. Revisit them regularly throughout your student's high school and early college career:

- How do you respond to feedback, particularly criticism that points out weaknesses?
- What skills come "easy" to you? Why do you think that is the case?
- What skill has taken you awhile to develop? Why do you think that is the case?
- What have you done for more than a year? Why have you sustained interest in that activity?
- Is there a skill you have developed through sustained effort and deliberate practice? What is it and how was it developed?
- Is there a skill that you didn't develop because you didn't put forth the effort? What was it? Why did you decide to give up?
- How do you work toward a goal that you want to achieve? What is your process in meeting the goal?

Parent Resources

Duckwork, Angela. *Grit: The Power and Passion of Perseverance*. Scribner, 2016.

Duckworth's much-anticipated book on her research on grit and resilience delivers both why people are gritty and how to cultivate grit in others. Her book provides research, stories, and practical tips that underscore the importance of developing grit.

WHY WE LOVE IT: Grit is a hot topic, and this book discusses how finding a purpose for your life and learning how to reroute around obstacles can help you develop grit. Chapter 10 is devoted to "Parenting for Grit," in which she provides advice on what she calls "Wise Parenting," the balance between being demanding and supportive.

~~~

Dweck, Carol. *Mindset: The New Psychology of Success*. Ballantine Books, 2007.

When someone says, "I am just not good in math," they are exhibiting what Carol Dweck calls "fixed mindset." Dweck's research led her to the publication of this book, which centers on the idea that people who embody growth mindset, rather than fixed mindset, are more successful in their studies and in life. Growth mindset is the viewpoint that effort, challenges, and setbacks are part of the learning process and those experiences should be embraced. Fixed mindset, which is the other side of the mindset coin, is the viewpoint that people are naturally talented and that obstacles and critical feedback should be avoided at all costs.

WHY WE LOVE IT: This book has changed how we talk to our adolescents, our students, and ourselves about how to handle life's difficulties; we have been cultivating growth mindsets ever since we read it.

Mindset Works® Website at
https://www.mindsetworks.com/parents/default

Carol Dweck and her colleagues provide resources that help parents understand the concept of mindset themselves and how to instill that mindset in their children. This website includes resources for parents to implement strategies at home and to connect your student's teachers on this topic.

WHY WE LOVE IT: This site provides practical, useable information and strategies that can be implemented immediately. It also provides guidelines for giving feedback to kids and young adults.

~~~

Smilkstein, Rita. *We're Born to Learn: Using the Brain's Natural Learning Process to Create Today's Curriculum.* 2nd ed. Corwin Press, 2011.

Smilkstein's work focuses on the learning process, and while her book's audience is educators, there is a lot to glean about how young adults learn best. Smilkstein's chapters focus on how neural connections are made and how differences in our ages and learning preferences affect our learning. The latter half of the book focuses on how teachers can harness this information to help students learn more efficiently and effectively.

WHY WE LOVE IT: This book describes the brain's learning process in such simple terms that students can easily understand the power of growing their own dendrites. Many students embrace this concept as a way to view their own academic challenges. Oftentimes, after a challenging assignment or course, they tell us, "I just grew more dendrites!"

Chapter 4
Successful students think critically.

When professors design courses, majors, and the other academic elements that make up what is called the "curriculum," they begin the process by defining what they call "learning objectives" or "learning outcomes." These objectives or outcomes describe what students should be able to do, understand, or know upon completion of specific courses and their overall major. While many of those objectives and outcomes are specific to each major, others are more general and apply to every student in college. For example, learning objectives that relate to engineering principles and techniques may be specific to engineering majors, but skillful writing and communication skills are universal learning outcomes for every student on campus.

One of the most challenging learning outcomes that professors strive to help students achieve is critical thinking—the traits, habits, and mindset needed to carefully evaluate an issue, question, or challenge from a variety of perspectives and with a range of considerations—before arriving at an opinion, decision, or action. Whether college students are really learning how to be critical thinkers is a constant debate in higher education, and as parents, you know that a similar debate is ongoing among adults who are trying to help young people become wise, so to speak, when processing information and making decisions. This chapter focuses on what you can do to help your student start thinking critically.

From High School to College Story: Sam

He wasn't sure why, but for as long as he could remember, Sam always wanted to join a fraternity when he got into college. True to his ambitions, he spent a considerable amount of time researching the websites for the various fraternities at each of the colleges where he planned to apply. Once accepted, and having chosen the college where he planned to attend, he immediately embarked on the path to "rush" his favorite fraternity, which is a term that describes the process that fraternities use to attract, evaluate, and select new members.

Sam can remember the exact time, place and date when he learned that he had been accepted as a new member of the fraternity. To him, this was the ultimate accomplishment for his college aspirations and a payoff for the work he invested in searching for the fraternity that was the best match for him.

Fast-forward a few months into his freshman year to finals week, when anxieties usually run high and the pressure builds. Sam and his fraternity "brothers" were in the fraternity lounge working in a study group, preparing for a grueling exam in physics, when one of the seniors in the fraternity entered the room with an announcement. Among the traditions and practices of the fraternity, there existed a physical storage file containing a vast collection of quizzes and exams that professors had used over time. This test file was a secret trove that fraternity members had gathered over the years and shared to help their brothers pass their classes and keep the fraternity's average GPA above the threshold required by the university.

Upon discovery of the test file, Sam's study group partners gave a resounding cheer and quickly began scanning the exams and quizzes for those given by their professor, who was known to be one of the most challenging on campus. Sam hesitated to join the frenzy. He wondered to himself, "Was this the right thing to do?"

To Think Critically Is to Be Inherently Skeptical

"Skeptical" sounds like a negative term. Why then, would we suggest that successful students should have this trait? We present the term "skeptical" because it implies that when a student is presented with information, he will, instinctively, pause and consider the possibility that this information may be biased, flawed, inaccurate, incomplete, or just plain wrong. Think about Sam's reaction in the story above. Was he pausing because he was skeptical of the appropriateness of accessing old tests? A healthy dose of skepticism in Sam's case provided him with a moment to think before he acted, to consider what he is doing and what the implication of his actions may be; in other words, Sam started the process of critical thinking.

Critical thinking is an essential quality not only for our students, but for us as well. We are in an era where there is a growing mistrust of information that is posted on the web or broadcast on television. Yet consumers in general, and college students in particular, are still prone to believe and accept content as true or authoritative when it's not. Critical thinking is also a highly valued workplace skill as more and more employers are reporting that they want to hire people who can think critically.

To teach students to become skeptical is not a bad thing. To be skeptical is not the same as being cynical, or naturally assuming the worst of people or circumstances. To be skeptical simply means that when presented with an opinion or a piece of information, the student naturally says, "This may be true, or it may not be true, and to know for sure will require more careful examination and research." That is, in its essence, critical thinking, and that is the habit of mind that successful students maintain during their academic careers, as well as their lifelong careers.

Going back to the opening story about Sam, his decision whether to use the content from the fraternity's test file to help him prepare for the exam will hinge, in part, on his predisposition towards critical thinking. If he has been taught to have a natural inclination to pause, carefully consider different perspectives and facts, and challenge what may seem to be the obvious best choice in light of what everyone else around him is choosing, he'll be in a better position to make a well-informed decision.

As observers, we want Sam to make the right choice, don't we? And, as a parent, you would want your student to make the right choice, also. But how? What can you do to equip your student with the habits of mind to become a critical thinker? Let's start by considering what critical thinking looks like in college, and then explore different strategies for helping your student become a more effective critical thinker.

> **Parent Tip:** Demonstrate critical thinking yourself. Your student is watching you, every day, so there are constant opportunities to demonstrate critical thinking in your decision making, opinions, and relationships.

What Does Critical Thinking Look Like in College?

Based on our experience in higher education, when is critical thinking essential, and what do we see in college as evidence that students are engaged in it? Let's start with the circumstances that require critical thinking:

- **When professors tell students to formulate an argument about a topic that is controversial or complex.** These are common assignments in college, and professors expect students to exercise independent thinking when making arguments, but also provide strong factual or logical support for the argument. For example, a professor may encourage students to state their opinions whether or not they believe global warming to be an actual phenomenon that is the result of human activity with the added requirement that students provide factual or scientific support for their argument.

- **When professors voice strong opinions about a topic that are in contrast to the student's own beliefs.** It is not uncommon for professors to state their personal opinions on matters such as religion and politics in class, leaving students whose opinions differ with an important decision—do they simply accept the professor's view as the truth, for example, in an effort to comply with that viewpoint, or should the student speak up and challenge the professor's opinion?

- **When students receive information that offers conflicting points of view or findings.** A college student conducting research on a question such as "Is coffee helpful or harmful to your health?" might discover some research studies that claim that coffee is harmful, but other studies that say coffee is helpful. How can a student resolve such discrepant information?

- **When students interact with other students whose backgrounds, life experiences, beliefs, languages, customs, and other characteristics are different from their own.** In other words, when students encounter diversity, critical thinking may involve thoughtfully examining their own viewpoints, beliefs, and potential biases. Oftentimes, it is our interactions with others who seem much different than ourselves that allows us to strengthen our curiosity and questioning of established thought, practices, and norms.

Parent Tip: Encourage respectful debate and discussions in your family. News stories and current events that touch on economic, political, religious, and cultural topics provide an ideal environment to share differing views, listen to understand, and offer alternative perspectives in a respectful manner.

What Can You Do to Foster Critical Thinking?

If these are the types of circumstances your student will face, what habits can he develop to become a more effective critical thinker? First, your student can regularly practice the process of *gathering* data, photos, videos, research, reports, and publications about an issue, and *evaluating* the quality and relevance of each of piece of information. It's similar to the process that a newspaper reporter or attorney would use in trying to write a news story or try a case in court. Each piece of information needs to be examined to determine its quality and relevance. For example, the results of a scientific research study would be considered more credible than someone's opinion on a blog or an editorial in a newspaper.

This ability to gather, organize, evaluate, and synthesize information is called information literacy, and it's an important learning goal at most colleges and universities. You've probably seen your student complete a number of term papers and other projects in high school that required research-related activities like this. In college, professors will expect students to gather information from more sources and to apply even more scrutiny to those sources before treating them as reliable. For example, your student may have managed to squeak out an "A" on a paper in high school by searching for sources with a simple Google search, but that strategy will not be sufficient in college.

Second, your student can purposely seek to understand and articulate perspectives that are quite different from his own. This is a particularly challenging task when the topic is very personal or controversial like politics, religion, and social issues. To become an effective critical thinker requires the ability to recognize different perspectives, respect the people who hold those views, and demonstrate that respect by taking the time to listen, study, and learn about those perspectives. In the process of learning more about other perspectives, your student will actually learn more about his own perspective as well and will develop a deeper understanding of complex and controversial issues. This is a valuable learning experience that will serve him well in college and life.

Third, and finally, is the process of presenting a particular argument, or hypothesis, and providing evidence in support of that particular hypothesis. Or, if the situation requires an actual decision, and not just an argument, this is the moment when a student makes that choice based on careful consideration of the options, the information at-hand, and different perspectives on the issue. In Sam's case, he might consider his choices (join his fraternity brothers and start looking through the test file or leave the room and study on his own), the reasons for and against each option (everyone else is using the test file, but it is clearly cheating), the consequences of each option (he could get a better grade by using the test file, but he could also get caught for cheating and flunk the class), and his own personal perspective (I want my fraternity brothers to like me, but I know that cheating is wrong), and then make a decision. If Sam has developed a natural tendency to be somewhat skeptical and to think critically about issues before making decisions, he'll be well-equipped to recognize that avoiding the test file is in his best long-term interests, and he'll walk away from the situation.

Let's revisit Sam's story and his dilemma. He decided to stop and ask questions of his fraternity brothers. "Are these files full of old tests that the professor provided to students as study aids?" asked Sam. He wanted to be sure he was not misunderstanding the situation. The answer was his fraternity brothers were not sure who originally gathered the old tests or if the professor was still using questions from them for current classes. Sam decided that because he could not be sure what the tests could or should be used for that he would not participate in using them to study. He also told the group that using them to study put them all in an uncomfortable situation of having to report academic integrity violations.

Sam suggested that the brothers either talk to the professor about the file and ask if the old tests were acceptable study aids or destroy them. Sam's stance wasn't easy—he knew he could jeopardize his status in the fraternity—but he had also taken the time to think critically about this situation and determine the possible outcomes. He chose the solution that fit best his values and that would have the fewest negative consequences.

Parent Tip: Emphasize with your student the value of hitting "pause" when you face important decisions. Few decisions actually demand instantaneous choices; you have it in your power and control to pause, consider the facts and alternative viewpoints, and then make a decision that's strongly rooted in critical thinking.

Parent-Student Conversation Starters

Use these questions to get the conversation going with your student. Revisit them regularly throughout your student's high school and early college career:

- Tell your student a story about a decision you made in your life that you regret (hopefully a story you're not afraid to tell!). Ask your student what you should have done differently when faced with that decision that could have produced a better outcome.

- Ask your student what major decisions he has to make over the next year and encourage him to talk about his approach for making those decisions. Don't critique, and don't lecture; just listen.

- Simply ask your student to explain what makes a decision a good decision and what makes it a bad decision. A key element here is that good decisions can lead to bad outcomes, but still be a relatively good decision because it was well-informed and thoughtful. It's the process of decision making and not always the outcome that determines the quality of a decision.

- When current events are discussed in your family, encourage conversation that presents and evaluates differing and conflicting viewpoints and perspectives. It's often helpful to ask what do those who disagree with your point of view think about this issue, and why?

Parent Resources

Hammond, John S., Keeney, Ralph L., and Raiffa, Howard. *Smart Choices: A Practical Guide to Making Better Decisions*. Crown Business, 2002.

This is one of the best books on effective decision making because it connects a trove of psychological research on decision-making biases and errors with a practical approach to decision making in the real world.

WHY WE LOVE IT: The book provides lots of practical, everyday examples for how to make better decisions, and the authors wrap the content with an easy-to-remember process they describe with the "PrOACT" acronym—Problem, Objectives, Alternatives, Consequences, and Tradeoffs. Students (and parents) who apply this model will naturally exercise their critical thinking skills in carefully considering the tradeoffs and consequences of their decisions.

~~~

Covey, Stephen. *The 7 Habits of Highly Effective People.*
Free Press, 1990.

This is one of the most widely-read books on personal effectiveness and improvement, and there's a reason why. It provides practical, yet universal, guidance on personal relationships and time and self-management for anyone, at any stage of his life or career.

WHY WE LOVE IT: The chapter titled "Seek First to Understand, Then Be Understood" offers some of the best advice on how to be an effective, empathetic listener that we've ever encountered. Why is listening so important for critical thinking? Because it takes effective listening skills to truly understand and appreciate someone else's feelings and opinions, especially when his views differ significantly from your own.

Chapter 5
Successful students embrace failure.

One of the key components to learning anything is using failure as part of the process. We know you are probably asking, "What? I thought this whole book is about avoiding failure and helping my student succeed?" Yes, this book *is* about helping your student develop skills necessary for succeeding in college, but learning to fail, or more precisely, learning to use failure as part of a development process is a key component to long-term success.

Call it mistakes, stumbling blocks, setbacks, or soft failures, but realize that your student needs these experiences to grow, preferably without parental interference to soften the blow. He needs these experiences to develop grit. He needs these experiences to discover his own way in the world. This chapter outlines how to help your student understand that failure is part of everyone's life story—and that we all can improve our outlook, circumstances, and situation because of our failures.

From High School to College Story: Ryan

As a young child, Ryan played soccer almost all year around. He was part of a traveling team and seemed to be a rising star on the field. When he was 14, he was scouted to play on an Olympic Development team, which meant he spent summer and winter breaks traveling far away to train with other up-and-coming young soccer players. He received many accolades from his coaches and teammates and once won a most valuable player award for his league. He enjoyed the positive attention.

When he started high school, he tried out for a new traveling team and earned a spot. However, as the season progressed, Ryan spent more and more time on the bench. His conversations with his coach never seemed to provide him with the guidance he needed to make improvements and earn some playing time. He felt at first that he was not working hard enough, but after several unsuccessful attempts to meet his coach's expectations, he felt like a failure. Frustrated by the experience, Ryan told his parents he intended to quit the team and try something else. He was convinced that he was not going to get a fair chance from his coach and his love for the game began to wane.

While his parents were concerned that he had not given himself enough time to make the adjustment to his new team and new coach, they did want him to try new activities and expand his friends group beyond his teammates. Secretly, they were concerned that he was spending too much time on one activity to the detriment of his development in other areas. Ryan decided that he would stay on the team through the current season, but he would quit playing for the league after that and perhaps explore an entirely different activity.

First, an Announcement about Failure

To make the most of this chapter, we need to be on the same page regarding the role that failure plays in our lives. We are all aware of the added pressure of raising children, especially today. The competition is more intense and the stakes seem higher in every way. We often worry that if we don't give our students every advantage possible, they will not be able to compete, to have opportunities, and to live a life of success. We also know deep down that they will be perfectly okay no matter what happens because our students are resilient. But we don't convey that second part to our students frequently enough.

A few years ago, Amy had a chance conversation with a young person who was attending a local university in Texas. She was in town to provide a workshop on college-readiness skills to the university faculty. This student, who was also her shuttle driver, confessed that he had really messed up his first semester in college and was working his way back to earning credits and improving his GPA. He knew it would be a long road to repair, but he had some words of wisdom that he asked her to share with the faculty.

He said that we (faculty, parents, society) use the word "success" too much and that while we mean well, we inadvertently create worry and anxiety among students about measuring up. Instead, he suggested, we should talk more about failure and how it is a part of the journey to success. Failure is normal and should be treated as such. It should also be used as a learning experience. This student's words have stuck with Amy. She offers them up as a reminder that we can all help by talking about the purpose of failure as part of the process and teach our students that everyone stumbles along the way and then works to get back up.

> **Parent Tip:** Talk about your own failures, what led to them and what you learned from them. Avoid overly negative admonitions by saying "Don't be like me!" Instead, talk about how the experience changed you.

Failure Defines a Moment, Not a Life

The best opportunities to learn often come from failure and disappointment, and the high school years can be a valuable time to start learning from them. There are many ways your student may already have encountered failure before he sets foot in college. You may have even felt disappointed with your student's failures. It is normal to provide expectations for your student to meet and to provide consequences when he doesn't meet them. Consider how your family copes when your student experiences the following:

- Doesn't get a grade you/he feels he deserves despite putting in the work.
- Isn't chosen for a team, group, organization, project despite doing everything possible to meet the criteria.
- Doesn't get any or "enough" playing time on a team despite attending practices.
- Doesn't receive an award that you/he thinks he deserves despite a track record of achievement.
- Doesn't get special favor, consideration, or exception regarding a policy, rule, or practice despite being a "good" student or person.
- Doesn't get to "redo" an assignment, test, or attempt to earn something after failing the first time or failing to submit it.

- Doesn't get invited to an event despite being friendly and well liked.

To be clear, we are not talking about blatant discrimination or an obvious error of omission that results in your student not achieving or not participating in something important. We are talking about the everyday decisions and outcomes that are part of life regardless of how hard someone works or what someone has achieved in the past. We can all point to events in our own lives when we didn't get something we thought we deserved, and yet that one instance does not define who we have become. That failure, setback, stumble, or mistake was only a moment and not the end of our life's story. It is important to remind your student of this as well.

The struggle for some parents, however, is avoiding the temptation to intervene when these things happen. Asking a teacher to allow your student to retake a test or asking a coach to reconsider a decision not to include your student on a team may result in a favorable outcome—your student retakes the test and earns a higher grade or your student joins the team—but the long-term effect may outweigh the short-term "victory." Your student will learn two things: 1) all decisions are negotiable and 2) his parents will intercede when things don't go his way. Both lessons will not serve him well in college and beyond.

> **Parent Tip:** Give your student space to make smaller mistakes or experience small failures. This could include not coming to his rescue when he forgets his homework, sports equipment, or lunch. Instead, give him space to figure out what he should do and how to avoid the situation next time.

Failure Helps Us Learn to Cope

Failure provides us with an opportunity to learn important life skills. College faculty and staff have reported that more and more students come to college without adequate coping skills. They see minor setbacks such as a low grade (think "B+") on a paper or test as undeserved and unfair; anything less than excellent is not part of their experience before college. Obviously, a world view in which perfection is the norm makes dealing with less-than-perfect outcomes difficult to manage.

We see this when students "shop" for classes that will be less demanding or when they avoid other challenging opportunities in favor of ones in which they have already demonstrated success. We also see this when students attempt to negotiate (beg, really) for higher grades than what they earned in the first place. In essence, these students often are unwilling to do the work to examine their shortcoming or setback and to honestly assess where they still need to develop.

Think back to Ryan's story. Although he had early successes on the soccer field, he never developed the self-reflection needed to examine what he needed to do better. Absent quality feedback from his new coach—which may be experienced in college as well—he was not sure how to adjust his skill development. Quitting seemed the easiest and best response.

At the other end of the spectrum is the student who sees very low grades (think "D's" and "F's") as an indication that he doesn't belong in college or that success will never be achieved. This type of student often holds views of himself that seem very different than a hyper-achiever's view: He doesn't believe that he will ever be successful, at least not in college. Some would argue that a student who sees low grades as an indication of failure demonstrates what Carol Dweck refers to as a fixed mindset, or the belief that one cannot improve skills and abilities through practice and setbacks, or failures.[11] Because of this mindset, students with a fixed mindset, too, struggle to cope with a very real part of the college experience, falling short of their expectations. This is a totally normal experience. All students find some aspect of college challenging and they stumble along the way. However, those who get through it see an opportunity to make improvements and redirect themselves.

Failure Is What Experts Do

Failure is an important part of the process of learning and can improve one's confidence. Why? Here is an example: Let's say you are working on some math problems and you review your answers. You realize that you have missed three problems and you start to go over what you did wrong and how to correct the process and get the right answer. That time you spent going back over the problem and thinking through both your wrong answer and how to correct it helped you grow those dendrites we discussed in an earlier chapter. Moreover, as Angela Duckworth addresses failure in her book *Grit*, "[T]rying to do things [people] can't do yet, failing, and learning what they need to do differently is *exactly* the way experts practice."[12]

As we described in the chapter "Successful Students Value Effort More Than Intellect," getting an answer wrong or hitting the wrong musical note helps develop neural connectors in the brain; the more and stronger neural connectors, the more learning. Failure can also help a student psychologically by building genuine self-confidence. Getting an answer right and not having any idea how or why you know it is right doesn't really build self-esteem. In fact, it may have the opposite effect and make you feel anxious about being an "imposter." Getting an answer wrong at first and learning why it is wrong and what to do to correct it can help you be less anxious about making a mistake and more confident about getting it right. It is the work that is put into understanding the failure and making changes to improve that pay off long term.

Parent Tip: Provide your student with ideas for working around short-term setbacks or failures such as earning a low grade or not getting into a club or on a team. Help him determine what he can do better next time or if the experience is part of a larger wake-up call to reconsider his strategies.

Failure Strengthens Our Grit and Offers New Pathways

While failure can help us strengthen our resolve, it can also reroute us to a better pathway. Let's return to Ryan's story. We can assume he received quality feedback from his coaches about his soccer skills when he was younger. However, it seems he ran into a setback with a new coach and a new team when he started high school and so decided to quit. It goes without saying that he would never be able to get better if he is no longer on the team. Nonetheless, Ryan used his dissatisfaction with the new soccer experience to determine that he wanted to explore other activities. He can use that setback as an opportunity to reroute to something else he thinks he would enjoy more. While this change of heart may make his parents pause, what sets this instance apart from failing at playing soccer is that Ryan can use the opportunity to find another pathway. Perhaps his lack of resolve in sticking with the team is influenced by a deeper desire to learn something new, cultivate new friendships, and satisfy a curiosity about other activities.

Failure Teaches Us a Lesson about Ourselves

When Amy's children were younger and they would earn a low grade on an assignment or they would make a mistake that led to an outcome they did not want, she would ask them, "What's the lesson in that?" Instead of dwelling on the disappointment or berating the kid for messing up, she would turn the focus to the debrief: what happened, why did it happen, what could be done differently next time? This redirection served the purpose of sending the message that failure is temporary, and it is a great opportunity to learn how to do things better or to make adjustments in strategy.

> **Parent Tip:** Talk about the steps for overcoming larger challenges, setbacks, or roadblocks, like not getting a part-time job or internship or getting rejected from a dream college. Suggest creating Plan B's for larger goals that are not achieved.

Failure Can Help Us Redefine Success

If you ask anyone what success looks like, you will get a variety of answers from "happiness" to "money and fame." Social media and television have contributed to our narrowing definition of success as well, for we see into people's lives with much more breadth—if not depth—than ever before. It is easy to get caught up in the race to have your student do more, achieve more, and be more if only to keep up with the other families whose students are high achievers. The drive to be successful, no matter what, has most likely contributed to increased anxiety in our young people and an inability to cope.

As your student navigates high school and the typical messages and experiences he will hear and see throughout those years, start the discussion of what success can and should look like for your student and your family. Other concepts of success can be for your student to support himself after he completes his education or training and be an engaged member of his community. The beauty of this conversation is that you and your family can co-create that definition. Just be sure to consider all the different ways that a person can live a good, satisfying, successful life.

> **Parent Tip:** Consider how you and your family define success. Is the definition too broad and difficult to achieve? Is it too narrow, leaving out all kinds of potential pathways for your student? Help your student identify diverse ways people are successful and discuss ways that your student envisions success for him.

Let's revisit Ryan one more time. Is his story about failing, giving up when the going gets tough, or about reconsidering his goals, pathways, and opportunities? One could say that Ryan's early experiences of success and the accolades that came from them kept him from developing skills in learning how to dig in when life gets challenging. One could also say that it is the new coach's fault for not nurturing improvements in a player, especially one whose interest and enthusiasm for the sport has been tempered by setbacks. One could also say that Ryan may have started to lose focus in maintaining the same level of development that propelled him to success as a younger player because he didn't love it anymore. Is Ryan a failure or should we blame his quitting on someone or something else? Viewpoint often determines what is a failure and what is a learning experience.

Parent-Student Conversation Starters

Use these questions to get the conversation going with your student. Revisit them regularly throughout your student's high school and early college career:

- When have you failed at something? What was your takeaway from that failure?
- What do you think is the most important part of experiencing failure?
- What setbacks have you experienced so far? What have you done differently because of them?
- How do you define success? What influences that definition? Can you imagine other ways someone can be successful?

Parent Resources

Lahey, Jessica. *The Gift of Failure: How the Best Parents Learn to Let Go So Their Children Can Succeed*. Harper, 2015.

If you have spent any time trying to shelter your adolescent from heartbreak and grief by protecting him from disappointment, you will want to read this book. Jessica Lahey makes a compelling case for why your student is better off when you back away and allow him to fail.

WHY WE LOVE IT: This book reminds us that students must fail as part of the learning process and it makes it clear that we parents can help students gain valuable information and develop skills for coping with failure.

~~~

Tough, Paul. *How Children Succeed: Grit, Curiosity, and the Hidden Power of Character.* Mariner Books, 2013.

Tough's book explores the idea of failure and success through the lens of character development. He focuses on perseverance, curiosity, optimism, and self-control and the researchers who are uncovering the science behind those traits and how they set children up for success. Tough interviews numerous people to answer the question "Why do some children succeed and others fail?"

WHY WE LOVE IT: Tough provides parents with an opportunity to learn from those who are doing the research in the field. The book offers numerous suggestions for helping students develop what educators call the non-cognitive skills such as grit and resilience.

Part II
Relating to Others

Chapter 6
Successful students build relationships.

Your student has had at least one full decade developing relationships and learning how to work with others—it is almost a prerequisite of kindergarten to learn to share, for example. Nonetheless, as she continues to develop socially and emotionally, relationships can get more complex and complicated. Dealing with raging hormones, pushing boundaries, experimenting with identity, and developing self-esteem can often collide, causing pain and suffering—and not just for your student!

Sowing the seeds of how to build solid relationships and how to deal with the ever-growing complexities of emerging adulthood is critical to your student's success as she moves from high school to college. To that end, this chapter focuses on the fundamentals of relationship building and describes what your student needs to know about creating and maintaining healthy relationships now and throughout life.

From High School to College Story: Alissa

Alissa has had few friends because she has always been shy and introverted. Although she participated in small group activities such as Girl Scouts and swim team when she was younger, she never made long-term, deep connections with others her age. When she was in the fifth grade, Alissa confessed to her parents that she felt anxious talking to others, which made it hard for her to make connections and develop friendships. On the weekends in high school, she would much rather hang out by herself than go out in groups to a football game or a restaurant. While her parents often worried about her lack of friendships, they supported her need to spend time alone because they knew it was her chance to re-energize after spending the week at school.

As she started high school, Alissa's avoidance of after-school activities and her withdrawal from the family worried her parents. Some of their friends told them that Alissa's behavior was completely normal and just a phase she would grow out of. However, her parents were also concerned that she preferred to communicate primarily through text messaging and social media. Alissa wanted to make more friends and be more communicative with her parents, but she didn't know how to do so.

Despite her intense introversion, Alissa developed a good relationship with her chemistry teacher in high school because it was easy to talk to her and she enjoyed working after school in the lab on chemistry projects. In fact, she was so interested in experimenting with chemicals that her teacher recommended she apply to a nearby college that had a well-regarded chemistry department. After a visit to the campus, Alissa applied and was accepted to the college.

When she began her college housing application, there was an option to reserve a single room, which meant she would not have a roommate her first year in college. Knowing that her parents would be concerned, she told them that she wanted to be alone her first year until she could meet people and find someone to live with that she knew. The thought of rooming with a stranger made her anxious. "What if she doesn't like her? What if they have very different ideas about when to go to bed or how to clean the room?" she thought to herself. Her parents didn't think living by herself was a good idea and worried that she would not get involved on campus and no one would be able to check on her if something were to happen. They told Alissa that they would not pay the extra expense of a single room and that they did not agree with her idea to wait until she knows someone well before rooming with someone. Alissa wasn't sure what to do.

The Most Connected Generation Can Be the Loneliest

As college educators, we have witnessed a variety of student development trends in our time, but none has been so pervasive and all-encompassing as the use of mobile phones for everything. It is not surprising to us as parents and educators that students such as Alissa prefer communicating electronically. Students have begun to rely on technology for a range of tasks from waking themselves up each day, to documenting their activities with photos, to listening to music and watching videos, to sharing all of this via the social media app of the moment. While we recognize the benefits of such technology, we also realize that taken to the extreme, there can be negative consequences: What can be a great advancement for parents who want to know, what, where, when and with whom their students do anything, it can also thwart the development of basic interpersonal relationship skills.

We see this on our own campuses: Students walk right past us with their eyes angled down at their phone screens, earbuds stuffed in their ears, and no awareness whatsoever of who is walking past them trying to engage them with a "Hello!" Couple this behavior with the regular confessions that our students make about being lonely and not feeling as though they have any good friends their first few terms in college. Many also confess to us that they don't know how to converse casually or delve deeper through discussions to learn more than surface information about another person. It is no wonder that some first-year students feel lonely early in their college careers.

Alissa's story is not that unusual, especially her anxiety about hanging out with others and developing friendships. But it doesn't have to be that way. Because of the work that we have been doing on our own campuses with first-year college students, we know that providing our students with some basic relationship-building skills lays a firm foundation on which to build a sense of connection to their colleges and to feel as though they belong and want to stay through graduation. These skills also help students feel more capable of weathering the typical storms of being in college. Better yet, these skills can—and should—be developed now so that our students have a toolkit of strategies for getting to know others and making new friends.

How can you help your student develop interpersonal skills rather than allow her to interact with others solely through technology? One step is to limit the amount of screen time (computer, TV, tablet, and smartphone) and create definite times to be completely unplugged. For many families, those times usually include meals and evenings. Another step is to actively engage your student in conversation by asking probing questions and listening to responses. For sure, we need to be unplugged from our own devices and distractions during these times as well. Finally, participating in intentional activities that don't require electricity can re-engage the disengaged: Take a hike, work or play in the yard, cook a meal, play a board game, build or create something, or do anything that involves activity, concentration, and interaction without the aid of technology.

Living and Working with Others Can Be Challenging

Let's face it: Living and working with others can be challenging no matter how skilled we are at building and sustaining relationships. Your student may already be negotiating the realities of living close to others by working through sibling and parent-child issues, but the game can change considerably when she gets ready to live and study in an all-new environment with, as some of our students have said with surprise, "strangers."

As Alissa's preference for living alone on campus reminds us, many people would rather avoid potentially challenging and unfamiliar situations if it is an option. While it may be comfortable for your student to ease into change, that uncomplicated route may also rob her of opportunities to learn new skills and demonstrate resilience in the process.

Even if Alissa convinces her parents that she needs to spend her first year living by herself, she will not be able to get out of every situation in which she needs to develop relationships with others. She will have new peers: people in her classes, her residence hall, her organizations and groups, and study or course work groups. Most of those people will be her age or close to her age, or "near peers" as we in higher education call them.

Your student will also have the opportunity to develop relationships with people who are older or who occupy roles of authority on campus. Professors, advisors, campus staff, and administrators are all people to seek out and engage with, not to avoid at all costs. The professor-student relationship is probably the most different for college students, especially after many students have spent 12 years engaging in a teacher-student (or teacher-student-parent) relationship, one that was authoritative in nature. In college, professors expect students to participate in adult-to-adult relationships (although the professor is still the authority figure), one in which the student takes on the responsibility of learning.

Your student will be best served by being comfortable using her relationship-building skills. How can you help? One way is to ask your student the following questions:

- How easily do you make new friends?
- How adaptable or flexible are you?
- How do you characterize your relationship with others in the house (e.g., siblings)?
- How aware are you of *your* daily habits, demeanor, and attitudes?
- How aware are you of *others'* daily habits, demeanor, and attitudes?
- How do you relate to authority figures?
- Do you know how to make "small talk"?
- Do you know how to sustain a conversation?
- Do you know how to ask for something you want?

- Do you know how to have a difficult conversation?

These questions are just a start, but they can provide a better understanding of where your student can build her relationship skills. The rest of the chapter explores some of the gaps that your student may have and how to fill them in.

> **Parent Tip:** Encourage your student to seek out opportunities to talk to people she doesn't know.

Dealing with Diversity Is a Real-world Skill

A student once told us that he was surprised to be in college classes with others who were old enough to be his parents. Because he mostly learned and socialized with people his own age—as K-12 education is organized—he was not used to working with others who were different ages. We recognized instantly that he was experiencing one kind of diversity our students can encounter in college, but there are so many other ways that a student body can be diverse. Diversity can refer to race; gender; sexuality; religious, political, and world views; physical and cognitive ability; culture; and, of course, age. College campuses are diverse often by design and, in some cases, much more diverse than our students' high schools. Developing healthy, long-term relationships means the ability to recognize and appreciate diversity—and even seek it out!

Being open to meeting new people who don't look like, sound like, or act like your student is a skill that can be developed, even if she is shy or uncomfortable around those who seem different. One way to help your student develop these skills and learn to appreciate the diversity of others is to model it yourself. Are your friends diverse? Do you make a point of speaking to others who are not like you? Do you seek opportunities to learn about others from diverse backgrounds? How do you speak about others who differ from you when they are not near? All of your actions and words influence how your student views diversity. Will your student be hesitant to reach out to others or will she be open to getting to know them? Think about what kind of model you provide for your student and initiate conversations about appreciating the diversity of the people around you. Your student views you as a role model for dealing with diversity.

> **Parent Tip:** Discuss the diversity of your family and friends as a starting point for expanding your student's appreciation of diversity.

Communicating Clearly Is a Key to Good Relationships

A key component to building relationships is learning how to communicate effectively. For a generation that communicates in text language and emojis, developing this skill may take more guidance and time. Think about Alissa's dilemma: She wants to make more friends and speak to all her teachers without feeling embarrassed, but she is not sure how to do that. Any communication she has with her parents or friends is most often through text messages. The small talk that is required to get to know someone at first makes her feel awkward and anxious. "How do adults do this all the time?" she often thinks.

As parents of adolescents ourselves, we know how difficult talking to grown-ups can be for young adults, especially those who are shy or uncomfortable around strangers. The more comfortable your student is introducing herself to people she does not know and comfortably conversing with them, the easier time she will have when she begins to make meaningful connections now and throughout her life. But also remember that becoming more comfortable meeting new people is a skill that can be developed. For sure, there are some young people who seem to be born with an outgoing personality and thrive in situations in which they don't know anyone. Debra Fine, in her book *Beyond Texting*, suggests that young people learn how to introduce themselves, ask questions, and give compliments as good ways to begin conversations with others.[13] At the least, make sure your student can do the following:

- Provide a clear, short self-introduction.
- Ask probing questions of others (e.g., "What has been the best part of your day so far?").
- Listen actively and respond to others' responses.
- Ask for clarification if confused or unsure of what was said.
- Express positive emotions.

As if building face-to-face communication skills are not difficult enough, the infiltration of technology into all aspects of our lives makes it easier to find other, less intimate ways to communicate. Alissa, as a new college student, is not alone in her preference to text rather than write an email or talk face to face. However, we know as educators that students with solid written communication skills are not only successful in college, but they are also highly valued in the workforce. Each new academic year brings tales from professors about the maddening and inscrutable emails that they receive from students. Let's just say that many students use "text speak" to communicate through email to professors, and the results often decrease effective communication. Consider the following email that a student has sent to a professor:

```
To: abaldwin@theuniversity.edu
From: partygirl999@party.com
Re: class
i was wondering what we did
during class and if i can make
it up i was sick from this
weekend LOL
```

Where to begin to describe what is wrong with this email? First, the email address, while not professional or academic, contains no information that would lead the professor to determine who is sending the email. There is no salutation such as "Dear Prof. Baldwin" or any indication that the student knows who she is sending the message to. Then, there is no information about what class was missed—the title of the course or the day missed. Professors often teach hundreds of students a semester through multiple classes. If they don't know who is emailing them from which class, the likelihood of a helpful response is slim. Finally, the use of "LOL," lower-case letters, and absence of punctuation as if the email were a text between friends will most likely not be well received. Professors—as would any other professionals—expect clearly written communications.

To that end, make sure your student can do the following in an email:

- Address the person appropriately. Use titles such as "Mr." or "Ms." or "Prof." or "Dr." with the person's last name at the top of the email.
- Communicate clearly the request or information.
- Use standard written English, conventional spelling, grammar, and punctuation.
- End with student's full name and additional contact information.

Even though students have complained about how much time and effort professional communications take, they need to realize that the people they are communicating with expect a well-written message. If there is anything we can do to help students develop high-quality, online communication skills, our work here will be worth it.

Conflict in Relationships Happens and Can Be Resolved

An integral part of building successful, long-lasting relationships is managing conflict effectively. And it is perhaps one of the hardest "adult" skills to develop because it often comes from having difficult conversations with others. The book *Difficult Conversations: How to Discuss What Matters Most* by Douglas Stone, Bruce Patton, and Sheila Heen provides a succinct template for building relationships on clear, honest communication and effective conflict resolution.[14] The authors suggest managing conflict by employing what they call a "learning conversation."

According to the Stone, Patton, and Heen, steps to a successful learning conversation include the following:

- **Starting the conversation with goal to create a "third story."** What this means is that you and the other person recognize that there are two versions of the conflict—yours and theirs—and that a third version may be closer to the truth.
- **Communicating curiosity instead of judgment.** Instead of making assumptions about the intentions of the other person, ask questions that demonstrate sincere curiosity. "Can you tell more about why you left the party without telling me?" is preferred over the accusatory statement "You left the party without telling me because you were embarrassed by what I said."
- **Aiming to listen and to be heard.** In some cases, you may never finally resolve conflict, but instead manage it and its aftereffects. In that case, your goal may be to listen to the other person and ensure you have been heard as well. One way to do this is to paraphrase or summarize each other's statements. Sometimes, a better of understanding of each other is the best outcome you can achieve.

If we revisit Alissa's story, we can see that her primary relationships are with her parents and her high school chemistry teacher. While it is obvious that she gets along with adults, relationships with peers have not been fully developed. Understandably, her parents worry that not having a roommate will rob of her of the ability to learn to live and work with someone her own age. It will also shelter her from the opportunities to learn to face relationship hardships. Conflict resolution is a skill to be developed—and when it is mastered, it can make building relationships a little less stressful—and Alissa's avoidance of a roommate keeps her from becoming competent in resolving relationship issues.

> **Parent Tip:** Talk about how to manage conflict through conversation. Practice good conflict management skills by seeking understanding, avoiding assumptions about others' motivations or intentions, and listening actively.

Parent-Student Conversation Starters

Use these questions to get the conversation going with your student. Revisit them regularly throughout your student's high school and early college career:

- How do you make friends? Who has been your best friend so far? Why?
- What is your biggest challenge with meeting new people?
- Do you find it difficult to talk to adults? Why?
- What relationship skills do you wish you had? How could you develop them starting now?

Parent Resources

Covey, Sean. *The Seven Habits of Highly Effective Teens*. Touchstone, 2014.

Covey builds on his father Stephen Covey's successful ideas in the original *The Seven Habits of Highly Effective People* by distilling the same wisdom, but in bite-sized chunks for young adults. He tackles topics such as setting goals, dealing with parents, and building friendships. This updated edition includes strategies for managing social media and dealing with cyberbullying.

WHY WE LOVE IT: Any book that speaks directly and clearly to teens themselves is highly valuable to us because it makes our jobs as parents a little easier. Covey's style is engaging without being preachy or too simplistic. Consider reading it with your student and talking about some of the strategies and advice that Covey suggests.

~~~

Fine, Deborah. Beyond Texting: *The Fine Art of Face-to-Face Communication for Teenagers*. Cannon Publishers, 2014.

Fine wastes no time spelling out the issue—teens could use some help learning how to communicate effectively with peers, adults, and even significant others. Her book offers sound advice for teens who may find it difficult to start a conversation or engage in anything more than small talk. She includes chapters on dealing with difficult conversations and managing online communication to enhancing face-to-face interactions. "I truly believe that in your teen years it's important to force yourself to do things that may be a little uncomfortable," she says. Fine seems to know her audience well and delivers expert advice for growing up and learning how to communicate effectively.

WHY WE LOVE IT: It is written in an engaging tone that is tough, yet supportive. If you want straightforward, practical advice that teens will respond to and use, pick up this book.

~~~

Stone, Douglas, Patton, Bruce, and Heen, Sheila. *Difficult Conversations: How to Discuss What Matters Most*. Penguin, 2010.

The authors describe how to approach difficult conversations to move toward resolution. Some of their key tips include listening without making assumptions, understanding how you and others contribute to the difficulty, and focusing on solving problems rather than placing blame. The book provides examples of typical professional and personal conflicts and a structure of working through situations productively.

WHY WE LOVE IT: This book is a game-changer in dealing with conflict through face-to-face communication because it gives everyone tools for understanding how conflict can arise, how *not* to respond (avoid making assumptions about others' actions and intentions, for example), and how to proceed to manage the conflict productively. If you put the authors' principles to work in difficult situations, you will become a big fan of this book.

Chapter 7
Successful students ask for help.

Asking for help is hard to do, especially if your student sees herself as independent and successful. Asking for help can be especially difficult for young adults who have been taught to do things for themselves. Parents can be proud when their young adult learns to do her own laundry, change a flat tire, and mend a broken relationship without anyone's help, but the downside is that this same young adult may become unwilling or unable to seek help when she really should.

Those of us in higher education encourage "help-seeking behaviors" in our students because we know 1) students need help even when they think they don't and 2) successful students know when to ask for help and where to go to find it. It is convincing students who are academically and socially capable that is the hardest part because they often don't realize they need help until a situation reaches a crisis. This chapter discusses the importance of increasing your student's self-awareness of her strengths and weaknesses, how to determine when help is needed, and how to ask for it.

From High School to College Story: Carrie

Carrie was a high achiever in high school. The only child of a single mother, Carrie knew the value of challenging work and self-reliance. She was a star math student and on the winning debate team for the state title. Her talents for logic and extemporaneous speaking made for a winning combination in the classroom and on the debate stage. While her mother worked two jobs for most of her high school career, Carrie spent her time volunteering at the Boys and Girls club teaching the kids to play chess or tutoring them in math and science. She loved giving back to her community and was a natural role model for the children at the club and in her neighborhood.

Carrie's self-confidence based on her high school years of accomplishments and accolades followed her as she began her first term of college. She was far away from her family and friends, but going to college was a lifelong dream for her. It wasn't too long, however, before the confidence wore off and she wondered why she had decided to go to such a rigorous school. When she realized that everyone else at her institution was a high achiever, self-doubt began to creep in. This seemed most evident in the classroom where her classmates engaged in intellectual discussions in class and gloated over high test grades. Despite her feelings of insecurity, she was even more strident than she had been in high school—she felt her pride was on the line—and she refused to seek out help.

She remembered that when she attended orientation, many of the upperclassmen talked about how much they used the tutoring labs on campus. It seemed that every subject had its own army of tutors ready to help. Something seemed wrong to her about that: Wasn't tutoring only for the weak students? She had never needed tutoring in high school and often fulfilled the role of tutor herself with those who didn't have the resources at home to do their homework. Her professors even talked about how to pass their classes and suggested classmates form study groups to work on problem sets together. Carrie knew she was not the "study group type" and found more satisfaction, even if it took her longer, to complete work on her own. She did not come all that way, she told herself, to rely on others when she was perfectly capable of studying without assistance.

By the end of the semester, Carrie was in danger of failing all but one of her classes. Principles of Speech Communication, Concepts of Biology, Introduction to Calculus, and Introduction to College Writing—all subjects she had aced in high school—had challenged her so much that she wondered if she was cut out for college. As she prepared for finals, and started thinking about what she would say to her family and friends once she returned home, Carrie felt defeated.

The Art of Asking for Help

Carrie's case is not unusual. She proved herself to be a capable individual in high school, yet those skills did not directly translate to college success in her first year. Although the circumstances may be different for different students, the consequence is often the same: Students who do not ask for help when they need it often find themselves struggling with their courses and feeling they are not cut out for college.

Why is asking for help an important skill in college? David Conley, a researcher on college-readiness, states that "[T]he students most in need of help are the least likely to pursue it on their own...because they don't know how to get help or they believe that accepting help indicates that they aren't college material in the first place."[15] Think back to Carrie's story. She was a stellar student in high school and didn't find much value in seeking help then because, quite frankly, she didn't need it. Besides, she had created an identity of self-reliance and accomplishment and asking for help may have made her doubt her own abilities. Had she been encouraged to develop help-seeking behaviors during high school or at least been given information about how common or even necessary it is for college students to use the resources that are available to help them, she might have sought those services without feeling shame.

> **Parent Tip:** Model help-seeking behaviors: The most powerful teaching tool you have at your disposal is the example you set yourself.

Your student may feel the same about asking for help regardless of her academic aptitude; it is natural to believe in self-reliance as a measure of emerging adulthood. The goal for your student, though, is to develop both self-reliance and interdependence through appropriate help-seeking behaviors. You can help your student develop these skills with the following actions:

#1 Help your student recognize her strengths and weaknesses. Self-aware students are more successful because they "know what they know and know what they don't." The problem with the transition from high school to college is too many students assume they are "really good" at an academic task—like writing a paper—and find out that those skills may not be ready for college just yet. To be fair, most high school students *are* good at high school, but they are not yet good at college, in part because they haven't experienced the unique demands. This is to be expected, so what can you do to help your student?

One straightforward way to get your student to know themselves better is to take a personality or interest inventory. Myers-Briggs Type Indicator or MBTI® is a popular assessment that identifies 16 personality types. Each type, which is represented by four letters (e.g., ENTJ, which stands for Extrovert, Intuitive, Thinking, and Judging) provides a description of personality traits that can be useful for understanding your student's preferences. Other common assessments include the following:

- Gallup's strengths assessment based on positive psychology called StrengthsQuest 2.0.[16]
- Neil Fleming's learning style preference inventory called VARK.[17]
- Angela Duckworth's questionnaire to determine resilience and "stick-to-itiveness" called the Grit Scale.[18]

If an assessment like the ones mentioned above are not available, you can also ask your student to assess herself on her academic, social, and emotional strengths and weaknesses. The results can be an opportunity to discuss strategies for making improvements. The goal here is to get your student to start the self-assessment, reflection, and adjustment process. She will need to recognize her tendencies and adjust for when she is away from you and thus must rely on herself to make changes.

#2 Help your student identify when she needs to reach out. In addition to knowing her strengths and weaknesses, your student also needs to know when she may need help. We *are not* talking about emergency situations that should be dealt with immediately. We *are* talking about those issues that are less straightforward. Issues that students often believe they can manage on their own, but that get them into trouble later.

Here are five common situations that you can help your student recognize as a time to ask for help:

- **Your student is not sure what the first step to solving a problem should be.** To get your student college ready, she should learn to identify what the first steps to solving a problem are. While each situation will differ, there are some common strategies for assessing a problem. Teach your student to answer the following questions when faced with a problem:

  1. What is the issue at hand? In other words, what is the problem that needs to be solved?
  2. How does she think it happened? Ask her what led up to the problem. She should be able to identify potential causes.
  3. How is she part of the issue? Everyone who has a problem has a role in it even if it is a small role. Help her determine her role and responsibilities. This is not necessarily the time to assign blame; instead, it is an opportunity to help her understand she has some power in the situation even if it is not at first evident.
  4. What are the possible steps to solving the problem? Work with your student to brainstorm possible solutions. Be sure to review the pros and cons of each possibility.

5. Which possible step would be the best one to start with? This is the step that requires deciding to solve the problem.

6. How did the first step or solution work? Always include an evaluation of the solution as a way to strengthen problem-solving skills. If the problem isn't resolved, go back to the list of other possible solutions and choose the next best one to implement.

- **Your student is confused by a task or directions to an assignment.** The solution, plain and simple: *ask*. If the task is an assignment from a teacher, it is best to ask the teacher. While a classmate or upper-class student may know the answer and can be the easiest person to ask, your student would be best served by going to the source of the assignment to prevent further confusion. For some students, this is hard to do if they are concerned they will look "dumb" or "needy." Or they may be afraid that they won't understand after talking with the teacher. College professors expect their students to come to them with questions. Many enjoy the one-on-one interaction and consider students who seek help as more committed to their work. Helping your student to feel comfortable asking for help now will provide her with a good foundation for communicating with her professors once she's in college.

- **Your student tried something that she usually does and it didn't work.** Studying for a test is a prime example. Consider this situation: a student studies 2-3 hours a day before a test and then fails it. That is when the question "Now what do I do?" arises. Usually the answer is not just "study more," but also "study more effectively." If the student doesn't know how—or assumes she knows how when she doesn't—then she will have difficulty making the necessary changes. In this case, your student needs to *ask someone who has expertise*. As in the example before, a classmate may not be the best source, even if it is an "A+" student. Your student will need to reach out to the teacher (or professor in college) or professional staff who work with students on academic skills when what she usually does is no longer working. She may not realize that her old ways of studying, for example, don't work well until she fails a test.

- **Your student is feeling overwhelmed or anxious.** A far-too-common issue that everyone faces at one time or another: being overwhelmed or anxious. We are not talking about extreme anxiety or panic attacks—those should be dealt with by seeking medical attention. We are talking about the everyday feeling that there is too much to do and not enough time. This is where the strategy to ask for help can be intimidating, especially if your student is asking for assistance in dealing with multiple deadlines.

- **Your student lacks the ability to create boundaries.** While your student may feel that she must make the most of her high school years by participating in multiple activities and attending as many events as possible, trying to do everything can be overwhelming. Oftentimes, students in this situation feel obligated to honor all requests of their time and energy. If you see your student falling into the trap of trying to please everyone or trying to participate in too many activities, you may want to start the conversation of how to manage multiple activities and requests. Learning to say "No" or "That doesn't work for me" are powerful ways to create a balanced life.

 # 3 Help your student distinguish what kind of help is needed and where to find it. What your student's school and community offer in terms of help for her will differ from one neighborhood to the next, but it is worth determining what kind of assistance and guidance is available. As a start, consider what your student's school already offers. Some examples include study hall, tutoring, before- or after-school programs, guidance counseling, and athletic training. Creating a list of services with your student can be a first step should a need arise. Perhaps if Carrie had thought about where she was having difficulty and why, she could have determined that regardless of her past performance, she needed some academic assistance. She could review what her college offers by talking with other students, asking her professors or an advisor, or checking out the college's website for academic services.

> **Parent Tip:** Learn about resources your school offers firsthand and discuss them with your student.

#4 Help your student use assistance appropriately. How much help is too much help? Should a student spend every week with a tutor getting help in her writing? The quick answer is that it depends. Certainly, in our 40 years of combined experience in higher education, we have seen far too many first-year college students not use the help on our campuses enough rather than become too dependent on that help. The goal for a successful student, and young adult for that matter, is to become *interdependent* rather than purely independent or dependent. Interdependence is the recognition that we must rely on others when appropriate.

Can you imagine a world in which you must change your own brakes, fill your own cavities, grow your own food, and reroof your own home? That would be ludicrous, of course, but often the conversation we have with our students is that they are becoming *independent* and will need to learn how to make their own decisions and do things for themselves. This is certainly true for tasks such as making their own appointments and doing their own laundry, but not necessary for everything an adult needs.

> **Parent Tip:** Before stepping in to help your student, find out what other help she has already tried. If your student is struggling with her math homework and complains to you or asks for your help, ask her what help and resources she has already pursued.

Let's revisit Carrie's story. Raised by an independent woman, Carrie had a good role model for self-sufficiency in her mother. Her early successes in high school, however, made her transition to college a little more difficult when she faced challenges. If she had more experience reaching out for help, she might have viewed the academic support services her college provided as part of the normal process of succeeding instead of an indication that she didn't belong there.

Parent-Student Conversation Starters

Use these questions to get the conversation going with your student. Revisit them regularly throughout your student's high school and early college career:

- What are your strengths and weaknesses?
- Is it easy for you to ask for help?
- If it is not easy for you to ask for help, what are the barriers?
- What do you know about the kinds of support available at your high school or college?
- Would you feel comfortable talking to someone you don't know about a problem you are experiencing?
- What can we do as a family to prepare you for developing help-seeking behaviors?

Parent Resources

Conley, David. *College Knowledge: What It Really Takes for Students to Succeed and What We Can Do to Get Them Ready.* Jossey-Bass, 2008.

David Conley has spent decades researching the factors necessary for young adults to be ready for college. In this book, he focuses on "college knowledge" necessary to connect the high school experience to college readiness.

WHY WE LOVE IT: While his audience for this book is broader than parents of high school students, it does provide insight into how the K-12 educational system is designed and what parents can do to maximize the experience for their students.

~~~

Fleming, Neil. VARK learning preferences inventory. http://vark-learn.com

Fleming's inventory assesses a person's visual (V), aural/auditory (A), read/write (R), and kinesthetic (K) learning preferences. After a 16-question inventory that includes questions about different learning situations, your student can determine which of the four preference modes they favor. If they favor more than one, they are considered multi-modal learners.

WHY WE LOVE IT: It is a short inventory that provides easy-to-interpret results. Fleming's website also provides specific strategies for each type of learning preference.

~~~

Clifton, Donald O., Anderson, Edward C., and Schreiner, Laurie A. *Strengths Quest: Discover and Develop Your Strengths in Academics, Career, and Beyond*. 2nd edition. Gallup Press, 2016.

A popular book on college campuses, this book provides an access code to take an online strengths survey, the results of which include descriptors of "top five themes of talent." It also provides practical strategies for further developing those strengths or using them in new contexts.

WHY WE LOVE IT: First, we love it because it focuses on strengths—and everyone who takes the assessment discovers her top five talents. It also provides affirming advice for making the most of those strengths. This book may be particularly helpful to students who have little awareness of what talents they do have and what they can do with them.

Chapter 8
Successful students help others.

In the previous chapter, we discussed how successful students ask for help. Now, we tackle the essential quality of helping others. For sure, helping others makes our communities better. Why, though, do we claim in this chapter that successful students benefit themselves from helping others? We believe, and the research supports our belief, that students who adopt both a helping mindset and service-oriented behaviors have a higher degree of overall well-being and are also more successful in their lives.

You no doubt yearn to see your student emerge into adulthood to become successful, but you also want her to be a good person, and helping others is an activity that fosters her character and personal qualities. This chapter outlines the importance of modeling service to others and supporting your student as she develops an awareness of the challenges of her community and finds a way to give back that fits her sense of purpose.

From High School to College Story: Jasmine

By the time she applied to college, Jasmine's resume was filled with hours of volunteer work and community service, including weekend volunteer work at the local animal shelter, summer camp leadership experience with YMCA, and community clean-up projects for the city. Jasmine knew that college recruiters would look favorably on this kind of experience, and it would help her get into selective colleges that looked for more than a high GPA and test scores.

Jasmine was successful in getting admitted to a selective college, and upon arrival, she quickly made friends and dove into the challenging coursework that her engineering major required. She considered the volunteer work and community service that she performed in high school as something she had to do in the past to get into a good college, but she didn't see any reason to spend time on those types of activities in college. She was too busy taking classes, studying, and hanging out with friends.

As the first semester dragged on, Jasmine started to struggle, mostly because she couldn't understand the purpose and relevance of the classes she was taking. She wanted to be an engineer, so why did she need to learn physics? Because she earned AP credit for calculus from her high school, she was placed in an advanced calculus class that was proving itself to be daunting.

Even worse, she had no idea how calculus was going to be relevant in her life and career. Jasmine was struggling not only with the coursework, but also with her sense of connection between what she wanted to do and what she was studying. What could she do?

Parent Tip: Look for opportunities that you can practice a service mindset, select a project, and set a date to work as a family. Be sure to discuss what you did and learned from it after the experience.

Instilling a Service Mindset in Your Student

When you visit college campuses with your student, you may have an opportunity to attend events, or fairs, that feature a broad range of centers, clubs, and organizations that provide membership activities and support to students. These types of fairs are common, and are a terrific opportunity for your student to meet students and staff from those organizations to learn firsthand about the experiences and beneficial outcomes that could be gained through participation.

One of the booths we encourage you and your student to visit will likely have the term "service learning" associated with it. Service learning allows students to directly participate in activities that are designed to benefit certain communities by helping to solve problems and offer support. It's a type of experiential learning that is very hands-on in nature and will often put students in contact with unfamiliar people and communities. For example, Engineers Without Borders is an organization that connects professors and students from various engineering disciplines with communities and organizations around the world who need help solving critical problems like access to clean drinking water or electricity through technical solutions like solar power.

In the chapter about developing a sense of purpose, we discussed the value and importance of helping your student make a connection between the academic classes she is taking and the broader purpose and significance of the skills she is learning from that class. This approach also applies in the context of service learning and other forms of helping others. Service learning can help a student see how the skills and knowledge she is acquiring and developing in college can be used to help others and solve real world problems that affect people and communities.

An engineering student like Jasmine might see, for example, how she can draw from her knowledge about thermodynamics (a class commonly required in engineering programs) to help residents in a rural village design a system to heat their homes that does not cause pollution or make the villagers sick. A business student, on the other hand, might see how his knowledge about accounting can be used to help a disabled veteran start a small business.

Service learning is one way for students to make the connection between their academic studies and real-world challenges and opportunities, and this connection has been shown to fuel motivation to help students persevere through challenging and tedious coursework. Jasmine's calculus class, for example, can give her the underlying mathematical knowledge and skills to help her design and develop products for those who are in need. If she can learn to look for those kinds of service-minded connections, she may have more resolve to dig in when the content gets challenging so that she can apply what she learns later to benefit others.

Research demonstrates that, under the right conditions and with the appropriate faculty instruction and guidance, service learning can transform a student's perspective by giving her an opportunity to interact with and help people who come from different backgrounds than her own and who face challenges and circumstances that the student herself may have never encountered. Furthermore, service learning is classified as a "high impact practice" by higher education experts because it has demonstrated tremendous benefits to learning across a wide variety of students and institutions.

> **Parent Tip:** When you visit colleges, look for a commitment to service learning or volunteer work as part of the college experience. Some colleges provide scholarships for students who agree to engage in a designated number of service or volunteer hours a week.

Besides service learning, there are other opportunities for your student to help others:

- **Performing volunteer work:** Religious groups, student clubs and organizations, including fraternities and sororities in college, commonly participate in events and volunteer efforts to support local causes and non-profit organizations. These activities help students make connections with the local community, and the students who participate have an opportunity to get outside their school environment to connect with people and organizations who need help.

- **Tutoring, advising, and mentoring other students:** Some of the best services for students are driven by other students; in college, that means student workers, peer mentors, student teaching assistants, and peer advisors. Why? Students can identify with and understand each other, in some cases to a greater degree than professional staff or faculty can. A peer advisor who is a well-trained upperclassman can offer a freshman excellent advice and encouragement about classes, internships, roommates, and other important issues that new students may struggle to understand. And, in the process of helping freshmen, the upperclassmen gain valuable experience and empathy. These same experiences may be available at your student's current school as well and can often be driven by school-sanctioned clubs or after-school programming.

- **Practicing habits of faithful friendship to peers, particularly during challenging times:** Your student may not have to look far for opportunities to help others. When your student goes to college, she will get to know her roommates, classmates, and other acquaintances and friends on campus, and she will build relationships with them over time. And, inevitably, those friends and acquaintances will need help. This does not always mean that your student needs to be the person providing the help, because the best outcome in many cases is for the person in need to get connected with professional staff, including doctors, nurses, residence-hall advisors, and counselors. In those cases, your student can still help by encouraging her friend to seek help, and maybe even walking with him to the health center, counseling center, or advising center so that her friend doesn't have to do it alone. No doubt that your student has already experienced a close friend who needs extra support during a challenging time and is starting to develop some of these skills that will serve her later in college.

- **Making connections with other generations:** An important contributor to a student's development and maturity is interaction with other generations, either older, younger, or, even better, both. Your family may include a natural environment for siblings, parents, grandparents, cousins, and older and younger brothers and sisters to interact and spend time together. When your student leaves for college, however, there could be opportunities for her to continue engaging with the elderly, by visiting local nursing homes or care facilities, as well as younger children, through local elementary schools, summer camps, and related activities. These intergenerational interactions open the door for your student to be more empathetic, kind, and helpful as a person.

These are just a few examples of activities that your student could participate in during college, either individually or through a class, student club or organization. In all of these cases, your student will develop a broader perspective about life, about others, and about herself, thus helping her become the kind of person you know she can be.

Parent Tip: Praise your student's strengths for helping others and encourage her to develop other related skills. For example, your student may be good at helping friends through a crisis, but not comfortable with working with the elderly. This gap in her skills could be a goal she could set to remedy through volunteer work at a nursing home.

Be the Change You Want to See

With an acknowledgement to Mahatma Gandhi's famous quote "Be the change you want to see in the world," we believe that if we want to see a difference in our community or in others' lives, we need to model that change in our words, thoughts, and actions. What can we do, as parents, to instill in our student a desire to help others? Here are a few ideas, with the recognition that this is not a complete list, nor is it realistic that we can put all of these ideas into practice:

#1 Model a service-oriented culture in your family and home. Life is busy, to be sure, and you most likely face competing priorities in your lives to manage your own careers, raise kids, and take care of personal responsibilities and obligations to your spouse and family. In the midst of that business, however, there may be opportunities to practice and demonstrate service through your church, school, athletics, homeless shelters, food banks, animal shelters, and non-profit organizations. If this hasn't been part of your family's culture to-date, it's never too late to start, and you can start with a well-defined commitment like a weekend event or clean-up project.

#2 Look for opportunities to talk about the challenges and difficulties faced by people and communities outside of your own. This isn't about making you or your student guilty about your prosperity and well-being relative to refugees, the homeless, or the disadvantaged; rather, it's about creating awareness about the issues that face all ofus as a community and as a society. A recognition of others' challenges develops empathy and can be the foundation of serving others. It can also help your student develop a sense of purpose as she embarks on her college experience and adulthood in general.

#3 Travel, travel, travel. You may not have the financial means to travel to exotic locations or far-off destinations, but traveling to other parts of your town or community, region, country, and other countries can be an eye-opening experience for you and your student. The simple act of experiencing different locations, foods, customs, religions, and cultures is transformative, and doesn't have to be expensive. If you calculate the total cost of parking, entry tickets, food, and hotel rooms for a family trip to an amusement park or the cost of staying at an all-inclusive family resort, you might be surprised by how far and exotic your travels can take you on this planet, particularly if you take advantage of youth hostels and other affordable living arrangements, or service-learning trips hosted by local churches, synagogues, or non-profit organizations.

#4 Affirm your student's passion for causes, and be patient and understanding if it's lacking. Some high school-aged students will, of their own choosing, become passionate about social, economic, political, or environmental causes. Your student's opinions and beliefs may challenge your own, but that's okay, and it's an important stage in the development of your student towards adulthood. These passions may inspire her to help others, as well. Your student, however, may not have this passion for causes, and she may not seem to exhibit this natural inclination to help others. In those cases, patience is warranted along with a good dose of setting an example in your own life for your student to watch. Eventually, she will find someone or some cause that she cares about and wants to help, and your patience will pay off.

> **Parent Tip:** Be patient if your student has not developed a connection to a cause; it takes time and experience to find a passion for helping others. Encourage her to start small (e.g., Provide water to those running a 5K) and continue to try new ways of giving to others and the community.

Let's consider Jasmine's story once again. She participated in service projects before college, but the current stress levels she is experiencing in her challenging major has left her little time to help others. She also finds her coursework to be difficult and disconnected with any real-world issues. It appears Jasmine may benefit from finding ways to connect her current experiences with her previous service work and to do so in a much more meaningful way. She could start looking by speaking with her professors. There may be opportunities to apply the work she is doing in classes to community needs or real-world challenges. She could also take some time to see what kinds of service opportunities her college offers or her community needs. Participating in even a one-time event could reinvigorate her and provide some much-needed motivation to get through her coursework. Such experiences could also help her recommit to her major and her career path by providing her with a sense of purpose.

From High School to College Conversation Starters

Use these questions to get the conversation going with your student. Revisit them regularly throughout your student's high school and early college career:

- What community issue interests you most? What do you see around you that you think should be fixed?
- What world issue interests you most? What do you see that should be fixed?
- If you could travel somewhere and serve another community, where would it be and why?
- How have you already served others? (No opportunity is too small to discuss.)
- What have you learned thus far from serving others?
- What could you study in college or learn more about that would help you solve the issue that interests you most?

Parent Resources

Brooks, David. *The Road to Character*. Random House, 2015.

David Brooks is an outstanding writer, and this book challenges his readers to consider the more enduring purpose for our lives by focusing on what he calls the "eulogy virtues" of kindness, bravery, honesty, and faithfulness that form a person's inner character.

WHY WE LOVE IT: *The Road to Character* draws on real-life stories of people like Dwight Eisenhower to demonstrate both the challenges and rewards of living out one's deepest convictions. It's an inspiring book, and sets up great conversations for you to have with your student about the person she wants to become, rather than the accomplishments she wants to achieve.

~~~

Association of American Colleges and University's summary of "High Impact Educational Practices" https://www.aacu.org/leap/hips.

This web page summarizes ten educational practices that have demonstrated through research to have a significant, positive impact on college student success. They include service learning, as we discuss in this chapter, as well as other activities such as learning communities and writing-intensive projects. Each of these activities is briefly described to help parents and students better understand them and their benefits.

WHY WE LOVE IT: Knowing about these practices can help parents and students become more informed and prepared to visit and compare various colleges and universities. It's a great guide to use when exploring a campus and a campus and its website.

Part III
Self-Management

Chapter 9
Successful students manage time.

Getting stuff done on time means not just turning in an assignment or completing a housing application form; it also means doing that stuff well when it is due. An on-time research paper can still earn a failing grade if it doesn't meet the requirements of the assignment. An on-time housing application form can keep your student from getting into a residence hall if it isn't completed correctly.

The truth about time management is that managing time is really about managing behaviors. It is also about learning how to plan and prioritize. If there is one constant that we hear from students each term it is that they wish they could manage their time and not wait to until the last minute to complete tasks; we also hear this from colleagues and friends who continue to struggle with balancing all the work they must do within the time they have to do it. This chapter focuses on why students often mismanage their time, and their behaviors, and what you can do to help your student build the necessary skills to conquer the stuff he has to do in college.

From High School to College Story: Jordan

As a high school student, Jordan ran track, worked part-time at a grocery store, and took "regular" high school classes. He qualified for Advanced Placement math and English, but he decided he wanted to enjoy his last two years of high school without the pressure of having to work too hard. He was a popular student, well-liked by his classmates and teachers. Even though he didn't find his classes particularly challenging, he completed most of the work on time. All through high school, he never worried about keeping on top of his schedules for track, work, and homework. Someone—either his parents, his teachers, his coaches, or his boss—was always reminding him almost daily what he needed to do.

Although he rarely arrived late for track practice or work, there were a few times that he submitted work late for school. He usually was reminded by his teachers that he had not turned in work, so he would turn it in a few days late for a minor penalty. His teachers, for the most part, knew he was smart and could do the work, so they often gave him leeway with due dates.

Jordan graduated from high school with a 3.1 GPA and enrolled in a university about 30 miles from home. He lived on campus and joined a few clubs as soon as he arrived on campus. Jordan enrolled in morning classes five days a week and was excited to have time to himself by noon each day. He did not work his first semester and spent most of that "free" time playing video games, participating in the clubs, and hanging out at the college's gym. He usually studied for tests the day before and completed writing assignments a couple of days before or the same day they were due, depending on how many pages he needed to write.

Around mid-term, Jordan felt that college was easier and more enjoyable than high school, but when he got his mid-term grades, he was surprised to see that he was failing two courses. He went to see his professors and discovered that in one class he had not logged into the online course management system to complete weekly quizzes. In the other class, he had not followed the instructions on the research paper assignment and received a failing grade. Shocked, and with just a few weeks left in the term, Jordan knew he needed to make some changes, but wasn't sure where to start.

Four Pitfalls of Time Management

Jordan's story is a typical one for new college students, and a good one to share with high school students who may find themselves in similar situations or displaying similar attitudes about managing time and coursework. In our work with first-year college students, we have seen time and time again the following pitfalls that can cause quite a bit of distress during the first term and beyond:

Pitfall #1: Students assume they can remember what they must do without writing it down. No matter how fantastic your student's memory is, he will not be able to remember everything he must do without writing down those tasks with some regularity. First-year college students tell us all the time that they can remember everything they need to accomplish because they were successful in high school, but high school teachers often write dates on the board and frequently give verbal reminders; coaches send out updates for practice and games (and usually communicate with parents via email or social media); and parents often set up an organizational strategy at home to help manage all the activities of every family member.

It is no wonder high school students do a pretty good job of remembering what they need to do—they often have a team of people helping them although they may not always recognize the integral roles that others have played in making that happen. Now, fast forward to the first semester of college. Those same students are highly confident that they can keep track of all of their tasks and activities, often by committing their "to do" list to memory. What they do not plan for is the number of tasks they will now be responsible for and the level of detail they must remember. A professor may ask students to read the assigned chapters, write a summary to bring to class, and provide some real-world examples of the content to illustrate what they have learned. Multiply that one task for one day of class by 4 or 5 classes over multiple weeks and it is easy to see how complicated your student's academic life can be.

Pitfall #2: Students take for granted they have (more than) enough time. A typical high school student spends about 35 hours a week in school. This does not include extracurricular activities or work/family responsibilities. Those hours are usually predictable and most times, teachers, coaches, bosses, and parents are driving those activities. There is nothing wrong with having a busy high school student; in fact, all of those activities and responsibilities are building skills and providing experiences that will serve your student well beyond high school. The issue comes, however, when a student has limited opportunity to develop his own time and task management skills. A heavy reliance on others to *tell* him what to do and when can make the transition to college more challenging when professors are going to communicate through a syllabus.

Additionally, there is a change from being *in school* from about 35 hours a week to being *in college* classes 12-15 hours a week. No wonder students report that they love the freedom of college! When they get to college, their class time has shrunk by more than half. What catches them off guard, then, is that while they are scheduled to be physically in class for about 15 hours, they are still expected to spend 20-45 more hours outside of class preparing for class, working on assignments, and studying for tests. It is easy to see that students who have not developed the discipline to do that work on their own will quickly be in trouble, especially because there are so many other activities that can serve as distractions to new college students.

Parent Tip: Get a calendar or planner that your student can use throughout high school.

Consider how this change in a student's schedule looks on a calendar. The calendar on the next page provides a typical 15-credit-hour schedule in which a student has mostly morning classes. The afternoons have no scheduled activities, although a student could have club meetings, a part-time job, or other obligations that could fill those hours.

For the sake of this exercise, let's assume that this student has time to study directly after the last class of each day. If the student schedules 5 hours a day during the week and 5 hours on Saturday, then 30 hours of course work can be completed *before* dinner each day. This means the student also has evenings and Sunday to do other things, maybe even relax!

	Sun 9/11	Mon 9/12	Tue 9/13	Wed 9/14	Thu 9/15	Fri 9/16	Sat 9/17
5am							
6am							
7am							
8am		WRTG 1310		WRTG 1310		WRTG 1310	
9am		HIST 1312		HIST 1312		HIST 1312	Studying
10am			SPCH 1300		SPCH 1300		
11am		PSYC 1301		PSYC 1301		PSYC 1301	
12pm		Studying	SOCI 2300	Studying	SOCI 2300	Studying	
1pm							
2pm			Studying		Studying		
3pm							
4pm							
5pm							
6pm							
7pm							
8pm							

One of the best strategies for helping your student learn how to manage time comes from the work of Laurie Hazard and Jean-Paul Nadeau in their book *Foundations for Learning*[19]. Hazard and Nadeau call their time management strategy the 8-8-8 Model. While it may be difficult to implement for high school students, the 8-8-8 Model allows new college students a method for ensuring that they add enough hours of studying each day to their schedule and that they get the sleep they need. It works like this:

- **8 hours of sleep each night.** This is a non-negotiable for high school and college students. In some cases, your student may need more (growing adolescents can sleep 10-12 hours a night). Your high school student may find it difficult once he gets to college to stick to a regular sleep schedule, and yet getting enough quality sleep each night is the cornerstone to managing all the tasks he will have throughout the semester.

- **8 hours of classes and course work.** This means that if your student attends three classes for a total of three hours one day, he will need to schedule 5 more hours of studying and working on assignments that day, and he should do this for each day he is in class. He may also need to spend that amount of time on the days he is not in class (read: Saturday and Sunday!).
- **8 hours of free time/family/work.** Although Hazard and Nadeau refer to this 8 hours as "leisure time," it may be more accurate to describe it as time that your student can spend working, participating in social organizations, volunteering, exercising, spending time with the family, or relaxing.

What makes this model particularly helpful for students is that it promotes a sense of balance and predictability in their schedule. Even if it is not a practical model for your high school student to follow, a discussion about how to use it—or how to modify it for high schoolers—in college is worth it.

> **Parent Tip:** Discuss the 8-8-8 Model with your student and try to demonstrate it yourself by balancing sleep, work, and free time.

Pitfall #3: Students underestimate how much time college-level assignments take. This truth has caused many new college students some stress as they stay up all night to complete an assignment that was designed to be done over multiple days, if not weeks. What makes this an obstacle for students who are transitioning from high school to college? One reason is that most students have mastered high school. What we mean by that is the habits and strategies that students developed in high school often served them well.

Think about Jordan's story: Turning in assignments late did not devastate his GPA; in fact, he earned a respectable 3.1. It is no wonder that many new first-year students assume their actions in high school should work in college. They just don't have the experience yet of knowing something different! That is why we feel strongly in helping you and your student prepare for college expectations, especially as it relates to managing time and tasks.

Let's take a 5-page paper that a student must write in college. A short assignment such as this can be deceptive because a competent writer could possibly write 1250 words on a topic in one day, maybe in a few hours. However, the assignment may require more than just meeting a page length. The paper may be a written argument that requires the student to explain and critique two complicated readings on a philosophical topic. Now, the 5-page paper takes on some complexity that may not have been required in high school because the student needs a clear understanding of the readings in addition to a defendable position about them. Let's add that the professor wants the paper to use a citation format that is unfamiliar to the student. Moreover, there will be additional time needed to learn how to document sources and ensure that proper format is followed.

See what we mean? This "simple" assignment now will take hours of preparation even before the writing begins. Professors who assign this type of paper are looking for thoughtful, intelligent responses that move beyond the obvious conclusions, and they may also be looking for clear, grammatically-correct writing that follows a specific format. This is a lot to expect from college students, especially from those who have not yet developed the habits of planning for the increased depth of thought and professionalism. Your role in your student's transition from high school to college can be to encourage more depth of thought and more professionalism in the work he does now so he can gain a sense of how much more time that takes.

> **Parent Tip:** Allow your student to experience "soft failures" when he doesn't meet deadlines. This includes getting tardies and detentions for being late to school in the morning and missing opportunities for field trips and special programs for not completing the necessary paperwork in time.

Pitfall #4: Students assume that some assignments are not as important as others. This statement reflects an attitude that can make managing time more difficult. Think again about Jordan's first semester in which he didn't complete the online quizzes in one of his classes? Had Jordan realized the importance of those quizzes not only to his overall grade, but also to his understanding of the content throughout the course, he could have developed a time and task management plan that would have included completing those quizzes on time. The best strategy for addressing this time management pitfall is to encourage your student to complete all assignments in high school, no matter how "insignificant" they seem to be. Of course, you may want to help your student prioritize if he doesn't have enough time to put appropriate effort into all of the work.

According to the students we have taught and advised over the years, time management is the one constant that seems to challenge them, especially in their first few terms. Regardless of their academic achievements or their high school schedules, college students find the shift from having most of their time managed for them to managing most of their time themselves to be difficult. Part of this difficulty comes from the fact that they are most likely managing basic life tasks in addition to college. Doing laundry, running errands, and even getting to bed at a reasonable time can be both exhilarating and stressful. That is why we offer this simple equation for managing course work. Here it is:

Quality work + timely completion = successful assignment

Quality work assumes that sufficient time is being spent. Quality work takes time and effort. Timely completion means that your student's time and tasks have been managed appropriately and that attention is paid to *when* it must be submitted as well. Too many new college students create quality work, but fail to submit that work when it is due. Doing both is essential to success in college—and the work place, for that matter.

> **Parent Tip:** Uphold the theme "quality work + timely submission = successful assignment" at home with chores and other responsibilities, such as doing laundry, cleaning, and preparing a meal.

If we revisit Jordan's story, we learn what he did differently after realizing that his actions in high school were not going to work in college. Jordan only had a few weeks to implement the strategies that we discussed earlier, but he did make some progress. He bought a calendar and began going through every course syllabus to determine what assignments he still had to complete before the end of term. One of the most important changes was altering how he spent his time. Instead of heading back to his room after class to take a nap or play video games, he went straight to the library to study for five hours before dinner. Finally, he decided that all assignments—no matter how few points they were worth—would be completed and submitted. These changes helped him to improve his grades, and now he offers the same tips to his classmates and his friends.

Parent-Student Conversation Starters

Use these questions to get the conversation going with your student. Revisit them regularly throughout your student's high school and early college career:

- What can you do to get regular sleep each night?
- How do you keep track of assignments and appointments? What modifications could be made to make planning more effective?

- How well do you complete tasks on your own? What could you do to improve?
- How do you plan for the unexpected and implement that plan with little stress?
- How do you handle most tasks or assignments that have multiple parts or deadlines? Do you rush through the process or do you take your time and carefully complete them?

Parent Resources

Hazard, Laurie L. and Nadeau, Jean-Paul. *Foundations for Learning: Claiming Your Education*, 3rd ed. Pearson Education, 2011.

Described as a text in which "students are pushed to consider how each mindset, perception, and attitude connects with their skill sets, and how one influences the other," Hazard and Nadeau provide research-based content and strategies to help your student develop successful habits of mind that will serve them well beyond the first year of college.

WHY WE LOVE IT: Hazard and Nadeau provide a wealth of information on the psychology behind specific behaviors that will help your student be successful. Of particular interest to you and your student may be the information about procrastination. We all procrastinate, but young adults often do not think through the consequences of such behaviors, so they often need practical steps for combatting the #1 killer of academic success.

~~~

Lythcott-Haims, Judith. *How to Raise an Adult: Break Free of the Overparenting Trap and Prepare Your Kid for Success.* Henry Holt, 2015.

Whether you are parenting young children or adult children, this book provides useful and insightful advice that doesn't make you feel ashamed or guilty about past parenting mistakes, but actually helps you feel more empowered and confident about the positive impact you can have on your adolescent as you prepare him for adulthood, including college. The author is former Stanford freshmen admissions dean and parent Julie Lythcott-Haims, and she provides evidence and facts about parenting rather than personal philosophies or anecdotes.

WHY WE LOVE IT: With chapter titles like "Prepare Them for Hard Work," this book provides parents with practical strategies informed by research to help your adolescent successfully adapt to the expectations and demands of adult life.

~~~

The Tomato Timer. www.tomato-timer.com

One effective technique for learning how to focus and complete tasks without distractions is called the Pomodoro Technique ("Pomodoro" is Italian for tomato). It is the simple method of setting a timer for 25 minutes and completing a task during that time. After the 25 minutes is finished, you take a 5-minute break. The goal is to repeat the 25 minutes as many times as you need to complete a task *and* to focus on the process, not the product. For example, if your student has a paper to write, he can set the timer and focus on creating a draft—not a finished, polished, perfect paper.

WHY WE LOVE IT: It is perhaps the simplest and most effective strategy we have taught students to use. And they love it as well. It is also endorsed by learning experts such as Dr. Barbara Oakley, engineering professor and author of *Mindshift: Breaking Through Obstacles to Learning and Discover Your Hidden Potential* (TarcherPerigee, 2017). Try it yourself!

Chapter 10
Successful students invest in their health.

As parents, we have invested a great deal of time and money to help our young ones be healthy. We've arranged doctor's appointments and therapies, prescriptions and medical treatments, participation in sports; we have also prepared a seemingly endless supply of healthy, balanced meals, all in an effort to support their health. For some students, their health is not a primary concern because they have lived relatively healthy lives. For others, their health may always be in the forefront of their thoughts as they live with the daily challenges of overcoming a lifelong illness or medical condition.

We also recognize that health isn't just a physical state of being; it's a matter of mental and social health as well. As you prepare to send your student to college, it's quite reasonable to wonder what health challenges and opportunities she will face, and how you can best prepare her for the transition. This chapter focuses on the considerations and strategies that can be instilled now that will help your student build upon healthy habits when she goes to college and embarks on the road to adulthood.

From High School to College Story: Jess

The concept of being healthy was a bit foreign to Jess. Her perspective on her physical condition had always been more strongly linked to her success in sports, starting in junior high and continuing into high school. Jess's concern wasn't about being healthy; she simply wanted to be in great shape to perform well and avoid injuries. Nutrition, too, was a distant concept that seemed irrelevant. Instead, she simply ate what she wanted, and when, to satisfy her appetite, which tended to peak during each year's training season for field hockey. She was proud of her strength and athleticism, and she felt justified in eating large quantities of food whenever the opportunity presented itself.

Jess was a good field hockey player from a high school perspective, but she knew she wasn't interested in playing in college, so she transitioned into college without any expectation of athletic success on a field hockey team. Besides, there were more important, and more interesting, things to be doing in college than playing field hockey. At best, she may play a casual game of field hockey with her friends, but she was not interested in playing competitively any longer. She had watched too many of her teammates suffer injuries that only worsened even after they went through physical therapy. Backing off intense physical activity seemed like a good way to keep from experiencing long-term physical issues.

During her first term at college, Jess's habits from high school started to catch up with her. Because she wasn't in training for field hockey any more, she didn't work out very much and certainly didn't see the need for it. She also kept eating as much as she wanted, whenever she wanted, but her body seemed to respond differently now, sometimes causing her to feel tired and sick. Soon she was starting to gain weight. Jess eventually realized that, apart from the practices and workouts that her high school field hockey coach would require, she actually didn't know much about how to take care of her body, and she certainly didn't have good habits in doing so.

Whose Health Is It? In College, the Ownership Changes Hands

Jess's story may not be like your student's, but there's an underlying premise in it that applies to every student as she transitions into college. That premise is one of ownership and responsibility. In high school, a student is surrounded by parents, coaches, counselors, and doctors who assume responsibility for that student's health, and they take that responsibility seriously. Parents and doctors coordinate annual physical exams and immunizations, coaches develop workout programs and practice schedules, and counselors initiate appointments with each student to check in and make sure she is okay. The student receives this care and attention with gratitude (most of the time), and simply shows up to appointments and checkups when told to do so. It's a good deal for the student and is probably the most appropriate strategy for caring adults to use, given the development stages of a young person in high school.

Fast forward to the first year of college. The parents are back at home, leaving it to the student to initiate doctor's appointments and checkups, and to follow any prescription regimens that are deemed necessary. Nurses, physicians, and mental health counselors are available in college, but their job is largely to respond to student requests, and not initiate those interactions. And unless the student is an athlete in college, there are no coaches planning practice and workout schedules for the student.

The ownership of health has shifted from other adults to the student herself and in many cases, the student doesn't recognize this shift in responsibility. In Jess's case, her health in high school was largely determined by the practice and workout regimen her coaches required, her annual checkups with her doctor that her parents arranged, and eating the foods provided for her in the refrigerator at home. When she arrived at college, she didn't recognize that the responsibility for her health was now in her own hands, and she was lost in what to do maintain her health long term.

We use the term "invest" in the title of this chapter to convey the idea that when your student takes time to exercise, rest, eat nutritious foods, and care for her emotional health, she is making an investment in herself that will yield rewards and returns over the short and long term. The shift in responsibility that your student will experience in college will require her to view her health as a valuable asset that can be used wisely or foolishly, with consequences for each. The college experience poses several challenges that will quickly test whether your student is inclined to take responsibility for her health and make wise investments in her well-being.

> **Parent Tip:** Work with your student to assess her overall health and develop health-related goals. Be sure to include strategies for decreasing the negative effects of stress as well.

Health Challenges and Opportunities for Your Student

As your student transitions to college, there are several important challenges and opportunities that emerge, which can either support your student's well-being or threaten it. These include personal freedom, the social environment, and the psychological implications of emerging adulthood:

- **Personal freedom:** Your student will have far more freedom and flexibility to manage her own time and activities, compared to her previous experience in high school. As we discussed in the chapter on managing time, the college student schedule includes class time, for sure, but also a lot of unstructured time that a student must manage herself. This time can be leveraged as an asset, including time devoted to exercise, rest, and healthy eating, or a liability, if the time is used to engage in behaviors that deplete her energy or are harmful to her health. The key issue here is that the responsibility for making those decisions shifts entirely to your student in college.

- **Social environment:** The social environment in college can be a significant positive contributor to your student's health, as in the case of classmates who participate in group study sessions or as workout partners in the recreation center, or a negative contributor, as in the case of roommates who bring alcohol or drugs into the residence halls. Roommates can be a source of tremendous support and camaraderie in some cases, but they can also be a source of tremendous conflict and stress, in the other, depending on the dynamics that occur between them and your student. Put simply, social well-being is a critical component of your student's overall health.

- **Emerging adulthood:** If your student is a traditional college-aged young adult between the ages of 18-24, the reality is that she is undergoing a significant phase of development and change that can impact her health. For example, most cognitive development research now suggests that the prefrontal cortex in the brain does not fully develop until the age of 25.[20] Why does that matter? The prefrontal cortex is the portion of the brain that provides self-regulatory behavior. It's the voice, so to speak, in your student's head that tells her to pause before jumping off a boulder into a lake before checking first to see how deep the water is. The reality of the college experience—and we don't tell you this to terrify you, but instead to paint a realistic picture—is that the college environment is basically a small town or city inhabited by young adults who have not fully developed into maturity, but who have been given vast personal freedom to explore life. Their decisions and behaviors will impact their health, either positively or negatively.

With the backdrop of these challenges, the next section offers guidance on how to support your student as she takes personal responsibility and ownership of her health and well-being.

> **Parent Tip:** Help your student advocate for herself in health-related matters. Encourage her to make her own appointments and be responsible for her medications, if applicable. Of course, monitor her progress along the way.

Health in College Is About Habits, Hangouts, and Help

Giving advice about health is a complicated business, and one could easily stray into misinformed or outdated information. However, based on what we know about the college experience and, more importantly, what we know about young adults, we offer three simple ingredients that most impact a student's health in college: habits, hangouts, and help.

First, students who develop and maintain healthy exercise and nutrition habits, among other components of a healthy lifestyle, do so by developing and maintaining healthy habits. Habits are crucial because they provide inertia and momentum to maintain behaviors even when, and especially when, there are challenges and obstacles. For example, a student who has developed a healthy habit of waking up at the same time each day and beginning the day with some form of exercise will be more likely to maintain that habit even during finals week when many other students are staying up late to study and then sleeping in afterwards. Habits are essential, and when students transition into college, they need to establish or re-establish habits that they know will help them stay healthy in the long term.

The second ingredient for a healthy lifestyle in college is the hangout, or where and with whom your student spends time. There's an old saying that goes something like this: "If you hang around the barbershop long enough, sooner or later you're going to get a haircut." What's the relevance of that quote for this topic? If your student spends a lot of time in locations that foster healthy habits, chances are higher that she will engage in healthy behaviors than if she spends more of her time in locations that support unhealthy habits. Cafeterias, residence hall rooms, bars, and restaurants are the types of locations that make it really easy to eat and drink beyond one's true appetite and avoid activity.

On the other hand, recreation centers, sports fields, and hiking trails make it much easier to be active and engaged. Similarly, the hangout ingredient relates to peers in college. A student who spends more time with peers who are, themselves, physically active and emotionally healthy will have more support and encouragement to follow a similar path for herself. If Jess wanted to maintain a healthy lifestyle without participating in college sports, she could consider making regular use of the gym or other athletic facilities on campus.

A third ingredient for health is help, which means that a student takes the time to know what resources are available on campus to help her be healthy and seeks help from those resources when she needs them. Taking the time to visit the campus health center and learn how to schedule appointments is a big step in the right direction, as is taking the initiative to visit the counseling center to learn about the available resources. The previous chapter on asking for help provides information on how to coach your student to become a strong self-advocate.

> **Parent Tip:** Make physical activity a part of your family activities. Instead of going to a movie or out to eat, consider making a family "date" to hike, bike, or swim together.

Using the habits, hangouts, and help framework, here's some advice you may consider to help prepare your student to take ownership of her health:

- **Habits:** Model the behaviors you want your student to practice: this is tough, but you cannot expect your student to exercise regularly and eat a lot of fresh fruits and vegetables if you aren't demonstrating that yourself. It's perfectly reasonable and understandable if this effort is a struggle for you and you sometimes fail because that gives you an opportunity to demonstrate how to recover from failure and get back to the daily habits without beating yourself up about it.
- **Hangouts:** There's only so much social engineering you can do to influence who your student hangs out with and where she spends her time, but encourage your student to find locations that will foster healthy activities, such as a recreation center, running, biking, and hiking trails, sports fields, clubs and student organizations where your student could meet

and hang out with like-minded peers who participate in sports and games.

- **Help:** Talk to your student about asking for help with health issues and taking ownership of staying healthy. This could mean taking proactive steps to remedy minor issues—such as a headache or seasonal allergies—and alerting you when she needs more support for making healthy food and exercise choices, for example.

> **Parent Tip:** Focus on fitness and healthy eating goals that are less about what you or your student looks like and more about what you or your student feels like.

How could these principles of investing in her health be applied to Jess's situation? First, once Jess finished the field hockey season in the fall of her senior year in high school, she could have established new habits to support her health, including regular exercise and a modification in diet to reflect the changes in her physical conditioning. Perhaps her parents could have altered the contents of the refrigerator at home to reflect the reality that Jess could no longer afford to eat whatever she wanted, whenever she wanted it. Second, Jess could have joined the track team to maintain camaraderie with her classmates and a regular workout regimen. It would have been difficult for Jess to develop a regular workout routine on her own after many years of prescribed workouts by her coaches and trainers, so transitioning to another sport may have given Jess some continuity in her fitness habits, as well as some new exercise options like running. And third, Jess could have sought help by talking with her doctor and high school athletic trainer to get advice about how to develop and maintain healthy habits after the end of her field hockey career.

A Special Note about Mental Health

According to a recent survey of more than 33,000 college students by the American College Health Association, about 38% reported that they had felt so depressed it was difficult to function, and approximately 10% had seriously considered suicide.[21] We don't cite these statistics to alarm or frighten you, but to provide a factual point of emphasis that mental health is an important consideration for you and your student as she embarks on her college experience. The expectations and uncertainties of the college experience, including the pressure to perform well academically, fit in socially, and manage the financial costs of college, can take a toll on students and trigger any number of mental health challenges that they may not be equipped to handle on their own.

In response to the growing prevalence of students' mental health issues, colleges have hired professional counselors and advisors who are well trained and equipped to help students navigate the emotional and psychological challenges they face as they transition into college and adulthood. These counselors are there for your student, ready to help and support her, but they can only help if your student is willing to reach out and seek that help when it's needed. Thus, when your student gets to college, the most important step you can take as a parent is to help your student identify the resources that are available on campus to provide counseling and other forms of mental health support and encourage her to ask for help.

Another important step that you can take to help your student is to take care of your own mental health. You, too, will be experiencing expectations and uncertainties as your student transitions into college that could trigger your own mental health challenges, or exacerbate challenges you've already been facing in your life, and these challenges provide an opportunity for you to take initiative, to recognize your own need for help and seek professional support and guidance.

By demonstrating that it's okay to admit that you need help and to ask for help, you are setting an example for your student, and equipping you and your family with tools and strategies you can use to manage the uncertainties, anxieties, conflicts, and stress that commonly arise during this important period of transition in your lives.

Parent-Student Conversation Starters

Use these questions to get the conversation going with your student. Revisit them regularly throughout your student's high school and early college career:

- What is your view of healthy eating?
- How could you include regular exercise into your weekly routine?
- Do you know how to handle minor health issues such as a cold or headache?
- What are your long-term health goals?
- Do you know how to make a doctor's appointment? Obtain a prescription?

- Do you usually communicate when you are not feeling well?
- What can you do to manage your emotional and mental health?

Parent Resources

Rath, Tom and Harter, Jim. *Wellbeing: The Five Essential Elements*. Gallup Press, 2010.

The authors present ideas and data that can inform you and your student about the five essential elements of well-being: career well-being, social well-being, financial well-being, physical well-being, and community well-being. The authors also provide guidance for how to thrive in all five of these areas.

WHY WE LOVE IT: Both you and your student are going through an important transition as she goes off to college, and this book provides an excellent guidebook for you and your family to reframe your activities, habits, and mindsets to ensure that your short-term decisions are helping you to achieve your long-term well-being.

~~~

Rogers, Holly. *The Mindful Twenty-Something: Life Skills to Handle Stress...and Everything Else*. New Harbinger Publications, 2016.

Rogers provides an easy-to-read, practical book on developing mindfulness for young adults. She focuses most of her chapters on mindfulness techniques to deal with stress; however, she also incorporates information about meditation as a road to developing a sense of happiness and satisfaction with life. Both strategies help improve one's overall health and outlook on life.

WHY WE LOVE IT: This book provides step-by-step instructions that meet young people where they are by not assuming they are meditating gurus! Rogers eases the reader into developing mindfulness skills and developing resilience to stress.

Chapter 11
Successful students manage their money.

When researchers and wildlife officials conduct studies of the fish populations in certain bodies of water, one of the techniques they use is to place an electrical prod in the water that temporarily stuns the fish and causes them to rise to the surface. This makes it easier for researchers to count and tag the fish. The topic of college-related finances is, in some ways, similar to that electrical prod because it causes a number of issues in our families to surface, and it can sometimes seem like a painful process to discuss financial issues with your family. For many parents and students, the question of how to pay for college and, once admitted, how to manage money during college, can elicit anxiety, conflict, and uncertainty.

Every family, and thus every college student, has a unique set of circumstances and personal histories involving money. Some parents can afford, and are willing to pay for, all of the expenses that are required for college, thus relieving their students of those responsibilities. Other parents cannot afford to pay for their students' college education, or they have intentionally chosen to put that responsibility primarily on their students. Neither of these situations is inherently better or worse than the other, but the parents in both situations share a common goal: They want to help their students learn how to manage money well in college and throughout their lives. In this chapter, we focus on how to help your student acquire financial knowledge, establish sound financial habits, and develop the discipline to make short-term financial sacrifices for long-term gains as she plans to attend college.

From High School to College Story: Dalia

Dalia's parents considered themselves to be neither rich nor poor; they saw themselves as a middle-class family with enough money to eat well, live in a nice home and drive relatively new cars. Dalia's parents didn't talk to her much about money because they viewed finances as their responsibility and a private issue not to be shared with the kids. Dalia grew up having most of what she needed given to her, but she also earned some of her own money through summer jobs that provided extra funds to go to movies and other activities with her friends. She quickly learned that if she didn't have enough of her own money to buy something she wanted, she could probably convince either her mom or dad to buy it for her. When it came to college, she and her parents never discussed the specifics, especially about the costs, and instead, they kept the focus on her getting good grades and performing well on the SAT and ACT.

When Dalia was out with her friends, she often had to borrow money from them to go to the movies or eat at a restaurant, and then she had to beg her parents for the money to pay her friends back. She looked with envy at her friends who had jobs and seemed to have the discipline to save money for what they wanted to buy in the future. She was starting to realize that she wasn't managing money well, but she wasn't sure how to get herself on track.

The Path to Adulthood Through Financial Responsibility

What does it take to help your student learn how to manage money well? We propose that there are four key lessons that every student needs to learn throughout her young life, preferably before she arrives on campus, to help her manage money well and make effective financial decisions throughout college and her life.

#1 Everything has a cost. One of the exercises we assign to our students in college is to develop a monthly budget for themselves, including income from various sources such as financial aid, personal savings, or family contributions, and expenses, including tuition, housing, food, books, supplies, and miscellaneous costs. Every year when we use this assignment, we see the same reaction from students, a mix of shock and anxiety, as it becomes apparent to them how much college really costs. In our conversations with first-year students, it's clear that many have not learned how much the basic essentials of life really cost, like rent for an apartment, a gallon of milk, or a laptop computer. In contrast, when we work with upperclassmen (juniors and seniors), they are far more likely to know how much these items cost. Why? Because they have acquired experience, over time, in having to pay for these items and factor those costs into their budgets.

As you prepare your student for college, you can help her a great deal by entrusting her with the responsibility to pay for the basic necessities of life—even if it's with a fixed allocation of money you provide for her with a monthly allowance—so that she gains direct knowledge of how much everything in life costs. It's one thing to complain to your family about how much a gallon of gas costs, but the reality is far more vivid for a 16-year-old who has a $50/month budget and is watching the dollar signs spin on the gas pump as she fills up her car. The lesson that everything has a cost is best learned through direct experience, and there are daily opportunities during the high school years for your student to gain those experiences by having to directly pay for what she wants and needs. It is never too late to give your student that experience, even if it's during her senior year or the summer before college begins.

#2 There are many ways to earn money, some easier than others. Once your student recognizes that everything in life costs money, and you aren't going to pay for everything on her behalf, she will likely acquire greater interest and motivation in working to earn money. A crucial issue here is that everyone has to start somewhere, and no job should be overlooked. Babysitting, housesitting, housecleaning, painting, home organizing, dog walking, pulling weeds and other forms of basic landscaping are all relatively low-skilled, entry-level opportunities that tend to require a lot of effort for a few dollars, which is the ideal learning laboratory for students to appreciate the value of an education. And, if your student has some skills and entrepreneurial tendencies, there are other income-generating opportunities, such as helping people sell items on eBay or other e-commerce sites, basic bookkeeping for a small business, or graphic design work on freelance sites like Upwork. Students in agricultural areas have other opportunities such as raising chickens and selling eggs, raising cattle in 4H and earning money when they are sold, and working on a farm or other agricultural-related facility for an hourly wage. Your student may need some initial guidance and suggestions to get started on these pursuits, but as long as she is sufficiently motivated to earn her own money, which you can help to stimulate by *not* paying for everything she wants and needs, she may surprise you by finding creative income opportunities.

#3 Becoming an adult means living within a budget. We all know that managing an entire household's budget over the course of several years, and a lifetime, is complicated business. There never seems to be enough money every month to pay for everything; the cost of everything seems to be constantly increasing; and no matter how much experience you have, there always seem to be unexpected expenses that arise, often at the very worst times. It's not realistic to expect your student to jump right into this kind of responsibility after graduating from college, so you may need to help her gradually develop the ability to manage a budget so she is ready for that responsibility.

Starting as early as elementary school or even as late as the last year of high school, you can entrust responsibility on your student to manage a specific budget for a specific set of needs and wants. It might start with a fixed budget for discretionary items like eating out, movies, arcades, shopping, and the unpredictable costs of hanging out with friends. The two key elements here are 1) establishing a fixed, limited budget, and 2) allowing your student to experience the reality of running out of money. You want your student to have enough money to eat and have the basic necessities of life, so the ideal learning experiences for budgeting can start with discretionary items, in which the consequences of running out of money are relatively benign.

Once your student gains experience in managing a relatively small budget for a concise list of items, you can gradually expand her scope of budgeting responsibilities to include gas, minor car maintenance and registration fees, new clothes, backpacks, and supplies for the school year, and funds for summer activities like camps. The key is to gradually increase your student's budgeting responsibilities so that she has experience managing a fairly complex budget by the time she leaves for college and recognize the important distinction between needs and wants.

#4 Delayed gratification is making short-term sacrifices for long-term gains. As your student gains knowledge about how much everything costs, learns how to earn her own money, and gains experience in managing a limited, fixed budget, she'll gain an appreciation over time for the reality that many of the items she would like to have or needs to have will require a patient, deliberate plan to accumulate money over time through savings. The items that often captivate the attention and desires of high-school aged students—videogame consoles, concert tickets, cars, smartphones, mountain bikes, and surfboards—can cost hundreds and even thousands of dollars, thus requiring a plan to earn money over time, save it, and accumulate it towards a large purchase. It's important for students to gain experience with the self-discipline and delayed gratification that this requires. However, there are two obstacles that can prevent students from gaining this experience and both involve parents. First, parents might step in and buy these items on their student's behalf, and second, parents might co-sign for their students to get a credit card. In either case, the learning opportunity is lost when students can take a shortcut to obtain what they want while avoiding the direct experience of delayed gratification and saving.

> **Parent Tip:** Make discussion about financial topics a regular event in your house. Talk about how much household items cost as well as your family values regarding spending money. For example, if your family values experiences and not things, discuss why you choose to spend your money on vacations or activities.

Surviving the Costs of College Starts with a Conversation (or Several)

Once you have set the stage for your student to understand money management and to develop skills handling her own finances, you may want to extend and expand those learning experiences beyond high school. Don't know how to begin the conversation about finances? Try these questions as starters:

#1 What does going to college cost? What we mean by this is what is the total cost of attending college, purchasing necessary supplies, living (on campus or off), eating, and taking care of and entertaining oneself. One way to figure this out is to look at colleges' cost of attendance information. It usually resides on the webpage that includes tuition and fees. You will usually see books, transportation, and personal items included in the total. While the accuracy of the information may vary from your reality, it is a good starting point.

- *What you should say:* Be honest about what it takes to live away at college. Food can be expensive (even if you are using a meal plan). Entertainment can be expensive. This is a good time to talk about wants and needs. Your student needs books and supplies while she may want a top-of-the-line gaming system.
- *Why you should say it:* If all you do is talk about the total costs of tuition and fees for your student's degree, then it is a step in the right direction. Take it from us who assign students to determine how much their total degree will cost, this information can be a game-changer in terms of helping students to stay motivated to graduate.

#2 Who is contributing what? After you talk about how much it will cost, it is logical to talk about how the bills will be paid. Your student may have family contributions, their own savings, scholarships, grants, and loans. We strongly advocate that your student has "skin in the game," which means she is contributing something toward the overall costs of attending college. This could be anything from having your student earn and save money to pay tuition, requiring your student to work a part-time job during college, or having your student apply for additional scholarships.

- *What you should say*: Tell her where the money is coming from and explain what she needs to do to remain eligible for the different types of financial aid. If she earns a scholarship, review the criteria for keeping it or renewing it. If she takes out a loan or receives a grant, remind her what she has to do to keep receiving it. Also, consider talking about the total amount of grants and loans she will be able to take. She needs to know that the metaphorical well doesn't necessarily replenish itself. This is also a good time to ask your student what she believes she should contribute to the costs. Remember, though, that your student may need some help figuring out that amount if she has not had a lot of experience earning money and paying for her expenses.

- *Why you should say it:* Your student needs to keep these criteria in mind as she sets goals for her academic progress when she is in college. If she does not realize that she must complete 67% of her attempted courses with at least a 2.0 GPA, she may think she can drop or fail classes with little to no consequence.

#3 What kind of budget do you expect for nonessentials? What we mean by this is what do you think is appropriate for a weekly "allowance" if your student is not working while in college? We have friends who have given their students everything from no money (They had to use their summer job money for anything other than books, tuition and fees, room and board.) to $100 a week.

- *What you should say:* This is where a longer conversation may be warranted. What do you expect that your student will use that money for? Is it to allow her to get something from the corner coffee shop or residence hall vending machine in between meals or is it to help her pay for transportation expenses from where she lives to campus? You should ask your student to come up with a list of reasonable weekly or monthly expenses and then negotiate from there.

- *Why you should say it:* This is a great opportunity for your student to consider her wants and needs and to learn how to plan ahead. We remember not going out with friends on Thursday so we could save extra money for Saturday night. While disheartening at the time, we now realize this was a great life lesson about thinking ahead and spending wisely.

#4 What will you do about emergencies? First, discuss what an emergency means to your family. For us, a flat tire or a broken laptop constitutes an emergency. A late-night pizza party for everyone on the floor at the residence hall is not an emergency (Trust me: This happened to a colleague of ours).

- *What you should say:* This may be where you define what an emergency is and what your expectation is for paying for it. Consider going through a protocol for handling the emergency. Will you give your student a credit card to handle it? Will you expect that she contacts you first? All of these questions should be answered in this conversation.
- *Why you should say it:* Things happen and being prepared for how to handle it when they come up is, again, part of the growing up process. Plus, your student will feel more confident knowing, for example, what she needs to do should she get a flat tire or her computer takes a tumble down the stairs.

#5 What are your family's expectations regarding continued financial support? What do you expect in terms of actions from your student? Do you expect her to increase her contributions each year? Do you expect her to search and apply for additional scholarships? Will you encourage her to work part-time to help pay for expenses? All of these questions should be discussed as you both plan for college.

- *What you should say:* If your student is on a scholarship or has taken a grant or loan, there will be expectations for keeping or renewing those streams of financial aid. If you are paying for some or all of the costs of college, you may consider asking your student to keep you informed about grades and progress and information she receives about filling out forms and registering for the next semester. She may need to be reminded that the college or university will communicate with her—and possibly *not* you—about all matters regarding financial aid, tuition payments, registration, and grades.

- *Why you should say it:* Setting expectations for your continued support or her continued enrollment is a vital part of the process. Unlike high school, where re-enrollment each semester was more or less automatic, college requires meeting certain requirements, meeting with advisors, and setting up payment plans or filing for financial aid on a regular basis.

If your student is still in the room and speaking to you after you initiate these conversations, then consider yourself successful! If not, know that you may have to circle back to some of these questions in time. She will eventually be grateful.

> **Parent Tip:** When you talk about college with your student, make sure the costs are part of the discussion. Costs include tuition and fees, net costs (tuition, fees, room and board minus scholarships, grants, and loans), living expenses, supplies, transportation, and incidentals.

Let's revisit Dalia's story. It seems as though she needs to sit down with her parents and begin a conversation about her situation. To help make her point about the need for some financial coaching, she also needs to determine what her weekly or monthly expenses are and how she has been paying for them to date. Moreover, she may want to research work opportunities on campus or nearby. She and her parents could then talk about the benefits and drawbacks of working while in college. Finally, she could agree to step up and take more responsibility for her finances—earning money, tracking her spending, and putting some aside for emergencies—and check in with her parents after a semester to determine what she still needed to improve.

Parent-Student Conversation Starters

Use these questions to get the conversation going with your student. Revisit them regularly throughout your student's high school and early college career:

- How much do you think _____ costs? (Fill in the blank with various items she uses frequently.)
- As a follow-up question, ask how many hours at a minimum-wage job would it take to pay for

specific items or experiences. For example, how many hours of work at $8.00/hour would it take to purchase a pair of $100 shoes?

- What can you do to earn money besides the allowance we give you?
- How do you determine what you spend your money on?
- What do you do when you find you don't have enough money to purchase something?
- Do you know how much college costs? What do you think a degree costs over four years?

Parent Resources

Sherman, Bob. *Surviving the Cost of College*, Stillwater River Publications, 2016

The author provides authoritative, practical advice to students and parents to help them better understand how much college really costs and what strategies they can use to manage and reduce those costs. In the book, he covers FAFSA and the CSS profile as well as net costs and tax deductions. Regardless of your financial situation or your knowledge of paying for college, you will benefit from reading this book with your student.

WHY WE LOVE IT: The book is practical and down-to-earth, and the author is experienced and well-informed both in terms of the financial aspects of affording college, as well as the emotional challenges that are associated with the college experience and its costs.

~~~

Kiyosaki, Robert T. *Rich Dad Poor Dad: What the Rich Teach Their Kids About Money That the Poor and Middle Class Do Not!* Plata Publishing, 2015.

We think it's a valuable resource for both parents and young adults to challenge their existing mindset about money. The basic premise of the book is that the wealthy are, for many reasons, wealthy because they adopt a different mindset about money and assets than those in the middle class. They purchase assets that can generate income, rather than assets that create further expenses. For young adults in college who are starting to develop their own financial habits, this book can be an eye-opener. We're not claiming that everyone who reads it will become as wealthy as the author, but we think there's a good chance that you and your student will glean valuable nuggets of insight from it.

WHY WE LOVE IT: The author provides excellent insights about money and wealth by contrasting two different perspectives, and the book sets up great opportunities for discussions between parents and their student about the important financial decisions they both face.

Chapter 12
Successful students harness technology.

Think about it: young people today were *born* into a connected world. They don't know how life was before we all had hand-held computers and cameras within a phone! They also don't know a life in which technology has not touched every part of it. Can't remember the lyrics to a song? Check the web. Want to invite a friend over? Message him on social media. Parenting, too, has been transformed by technology. Concerned your student is failing English? Check his grades online. Want to know exactly where your student is at 9 p.m. on a Friday? Use a GPS location service. No doubt, we will soon not be able to think about raising kids without the benefits (and sometimes drawbacks) of technology.

There's no escaping the reality that technology plays an important role in the life of your student, and its role can have both positive and negative effects on his success and well-being. Thus, it's important to anticipate both the challenges and opportunities that your student will experience in college relating to technology so that you can play a positive and supportive role in your student's success. To be successful, your student will need to be proficient with various apps and software without allowing the technology to overcome him. Our use of the term "harness technology" is intentional, to convey the idea that technology is a powerful tool, but needs to be managed and restrained. This chapter outlines how to help your student use technology to support his success.

From High School to College Story: Omar

Omar was, in every sense of the word, a digital native. He grew up with computers, saved his own money to buy a smartphone when he was quite young, and proved himself adept at learning new technologies and helping his family members who weren't quite as proficient. His parents lovingly referred to him as their "in-home tech support."

When Omar moved into his residence hall in college, he spent most of the first few days unpacking, assembling, and configuring his technology—even before unpacking his clothes. By the time classes started the first week, Omar had his smartphone, laptop, tablet, videogame console, and wearables all set up and configured to access the college's network, and he started where he left off in high school by communicating almost constantly with his friends and family through Snapchat, text messages, and WhatsApp. His roommate and residence hall companions quickly adopted Omar as their go-to guy to handle their own technical problems, and Omar's dorm room was the place to be for epic videogame battles and discussions about the latest and greatest technologies and coding tricks for jailbreaking smartphones and cheats for videogames.

It wasn't until midway through the semester that Omar's roommate started to complain to the residence hall staff about Omar's late nights and loud visitors in the room. Omar was skipping classes, choosing instead to monitor class activity through the college's learning management system; he also tried to keep up with what was going on in class through chat sessions with his classmates and friends. Although he felt connected, the reality was that Omar was spending less and less time in direct contact with people. For Omar, the growing isolation seemed subtle and he barely noticed it. But his roommate recognized that the situation was getting worse, and the roommate wasn't exactly sure what, if anything, residence hall staff could do other than talk to him about limiting visitors. Omar really needed to find a better balance with using technology and making the most of his college experience.

What Technology Gives, It Can Also Take Away

As Omar's story demonstrates, what makes technology appealing and useful can also make it distracting and detrimental. For sure, technology can be a double-edged sword as its benefits can be, when taken to an extreme, its downsides as well. Technology, especially our smartphones, have given us the ability to do the following:

- **Connect with others regardless of time and distance and yet still be lonely.** This advantage has allowed us to know what our childhood friends are doing right this minute, even if the last time we talked to them was in Mrs. McCain's second-grade math class. More importantly, it has made the distances that some families endure a little easier by bringing us together through voice and text in real time. However, this ability to connect with just about anyone anywhere has also made disconnection easier. What passes as a relationship these days can sometimes be only a series of short texts or tweets that amount to shallow exchange of information.

- **Find information in little-to-no time and yet remain ignorant of many subjects.** Ever struggle to remember the actor who played the father in that television show from the 1970s? Well, you don't have to wonder anymore now that the whole world of information is at the tip of our fingers. The Internet and search engines have brought us more information than we would ever have time to read and even more is being generated each second. This ability to know just about everything at the blink of an eye also makes it easier to be a master of none. In other words, our knowledge of many subjects can be a mile wide and an inch deep, making us think we know more than we really do.

- **Communicate our thoughts immediately and yet find ourselves miscommunicating or worse.** Text, email, and social media have allowed us to record instantaneously what we are thinking, feeling, and doing. No time in history have we been able to read and record so many people's actions and musings, and yet this ability to communicate has led to some to take it to the extreme. "Trolling" on sites to express displeasure about a topic and then subsequently displeasure at others can—and has—led to bullying and even worse.

- **Enjoy entertainment anytime, anywhere and yet feel restless and bored.** At its most innocent, technology has provided us with the ability to be entertained through funny videos and mashed-up photos and memes and access to our favorite music, television shows, and movies. However, this constant access and need to be entertained has made it more difficult for us to learn to entertain ourselves by ourselves or to use our imagination productively.

> **Parent Tip:** Your student can learn to thrive in boredom because he must create his own fun or follow his own curiosities about the world around him. Build in more technology downtime in your family's day-to-day schedule.

Getting Ready for Using Technology in College

Regardless of whether or not his story resembles your student's, Omar's story provides context to discuss both the opportunities and challenges that today's college students—and your student—will face as he embarks on his college experience. To be successful in college and his career, your student will need to develop a sufficient aptitude with various forms of technology to take advantage of these opportunities. Looking beyond graduation, technology will also play a key role in his career so his accomplishments in learning how to use technology effectively in college will have long-term benefits.

As we discussed above, technology brings benefits and drawbacks when taken to the extreme; for example, it can be a great source of information and support for your student, but it can also become detrimental to your student's success as Omar's story demonstrates. Here are some of the most significant challenges we see with technology for students based on our experience in working in higher education:

#1 Technology costs money, and those costs tend to recur. Most of the devices, apps, and software needed for college courses tend to cost money to purchase, download, and use, and the constant drumbeat of new versions and upgrades creates continual pressure for ongoing investments to keep everything up-to-date and performing well. Many of us have grown so used to the monthly costs of data plans and subscriptions that we fail to recognize how much we spend on an annual basis as a family on technology. And many of the in-app purchases and downloads are small, automatic transactions that can build up over time without you or your student noticing them.

#2 Technology can save time, but it also consumes time. Researching, purchasing, configuring, downloading, updating, and maintaining devices, apps, and software can be a black hole of time. And these activities aren't even the most time-consuming element; learning to use the technology and using it on an ongoing basis can be time consuming. College students can easily lose track of how much time they are spending on technology-related activities, many of which are not directly related to their academic pursuits or productivity.

#3 Technology can prove to be a constant source of distraction and interruption. We expect that many parents who read this will already recognize how distracted people are with their smartphones, wearables, and other devices, and it's easy to see how a student who is continually tempted to look at his phone every time it vibrates or pings may have a difficult time staying focused on the hard work, and sometimes tedious work, that learning and studying requires.

#4 Technology is a litmus test of personal integrity. Having access to vast sources of information on a device that fits in the palm of the hand is exciting and powerful, but it also delivers a compelling temptation to cheat. We'll just be blunt here and say that cheating is wrong, and it's wrong for two reasons. First, cheating is a violation of a college's academic integrity policies and second, cheating degrades real learning. If your student chooses to take the risk of cheating in college by utilizing technology, he runs a very real risk of incurring serious consequences. College students might share a laugh about how naïve they think their professor is, but the vast majority of the faculty we know are quite savvy, and many have developed methods for detecting and dealing with cheating by using methods that students may be completely unaware of.

This issue of integrity also relates to pirated and unlicensed software, illegal music and movie downloads, and unauthorized sharing of paid subscriptions and services between students. There is a pervasive mentality that because they are students and have minimal financial resources, they are justified in downloading software illegally or piggybacking on someone else's paid subscription to a service to avoid paying for it themselves. Such decisions carry short-term risks of being caught and punished (when these activities occur on a college network they violate the college's information technology policies and can carry significant consequences), as well as the long-term implications of undermining your student's personal integrity.

#5 Technology carries risks associated with a student's privacy, security and safety. The public is becoming increasingly informed about the amount of data and information that technology providers are collecting, analyzing and selling for commercial gain. Furthermore, public awareness is growing about the risks of cyber-attacks, identify theft, and invasions of privacy through unauthorized access to personal information, photos, video cameras on devices, and tracking software. All of these carry risks to your student's privacy, financial security, and physical safety.

#6 Overuse and misuse of technology carry social implications. The time that a student invests in the use of technology is time not spent interacting socially with others, exercising, building relationships, and practicing social skills that are essential for success and well-being in his career and life. Thus, there is a significant opportunity cost that a student incurs when he spends countless hours with his devices.

College students can also incur significant negative consequences to their reputation and career prospects through the misuse of technology. Embarrassing photos and videos of your student, taken by others, can easily be posted and permanently retained on the Internet through social media, leading to a lifetime of unintended consequences and regrets. And corporate recruiters are increasingly relying on an audit of a prospect's social media presence to determine whether to extend a job offer or not.

> **Parent Tip:** Monitor your student's use of technology and ask questions to see if he understands how to use it safely and ethically.

Plug into the Technology Yourself

Now that we've scared you with all of the problems your student can experience because of the misuse or overuse of technology, what are you to do? The obvious choice, of course, is to move your entire family to a rural outpost with no access to electricity or the Internet, spending your days and hours tilling the soil and handwashing clothes! Okay, maybe there is a happy medium here to help you and your student deal with technology use in a calm, thoughtful manner.

#1 Set the example. The first thing we need to recognize is that our own choices and behaviors around technology provide the strongest reference point for a family to consider. Yes, we realize that your student's peers have a tremendous impact on his choices, and once he is off to college, he won't observe your own behavior as much. However, if you still have some time with your student before he leaves for college, you can revisit your own habits relating to technology and make adjustments as needed. Before lecturing about spending too much time with his devices, consider how much time he sees you spending with a phone in your hand or next to your ear. Plus, by placing an expectation on your student to respond quickly to texts, emails, and social media posts, there is an expectation for him to develop the habit of constant use and distraction.

#2 Be vigilant, but not terrified. Your student does have a learning curve he needs to engage to become savvy about protecting his username and passwords and thinking carefully about his social media posts and downloads. But if fears about the risks he faces in using technology cause you to become hysterical and paranoid, there is a risk that your student will start to ignore you altogether or purposely defy your advice with even riskier behavior. We realize that this may be getting rather personal regarding the relational and social dynamics in your own home, but we are trying to be helpful by suggesting that you offer insights and advice in a manner that does not cause emotions to overwhelm the rational aspects of your guidance.

#3 Define, discuss, and enforce limits, expectations, and consequences. While your student is living at home, and if you help pay for his technology when he is in college, you have the authority and ability to establish limits. There are a number of apps and other technologies that empower parents to track usage and enforce limits, and you are quite justified in imposing these on behalf of your student's well-being. And if he violates the limits that you establish, you'll need to impose consequences, such as a temporary suspension or reduction of his data plan, or payment from him for any overage charges (if he goes over the reduced data plan) to encourage the kind of learning that life experiences and consequences can facilitate.

#4 Establish and maintain boundaries. In the zeal to protect, parents can sometimes go too far in their efforts to monitor and influence their student's use of technology. One example is when parents require their student to share usernames and passwords to school accounts so that they can access email traffic, grades, and other school-related data. While this practice may be fine for students who are under 18, that is not the case in higher education. In fact, providing a parent or anyone else with a username and password, or access to software programs run by the institution, is actually a breach of most college technology use policies and your student would suffer the consequences. It's also a violation of the federal law around student privacy called the Family Educational Rights and Privacy Act (FERPA), which protects the records and information of students who are enrolled at a college or university. Parents may also go too far if they constantly "troll" their student's social media activity, constantly watching for anything inappropriate or troubling. There comes a time in a student's life and his progression towards maturity in which he deserves some degree of autonomy and privacy outside his parent's gazing eyes to make his own choices about how he manages technology. We can inform, warn, and set limits to the degree we feel is appropriate, but there are boundaries we should not cross because we want to help our student transition towards independence and self-control.

> **Parent Tip:** Strike a balance between keeping an eye on your student's use of technology through the use of it yourself or other technology designed to help you monitor your student. However, find ways to provide opportunities for your student to take ownership of the choices he makes with technology and provide natural consequences should he make mistakes.

Let's go back to Omar and re-examine his story. The fact that he is naturally predisposed to technology—and quite good at it—makes this a complicated situation. On the one hand, his parents wanted to encourage his learning and skill development with technology because of the obvious potential career opportunities that he could pursue with those skills. On the other hand, his parents also wanted Omar to develop healthy relationships with people through means other than social media and to spend time on other activities like sports or volunteering. Imposing some kind of limits on his technology use and access while living at home would have been justified.

However, if we can't hit the rewind button on the story about Omar and change how his parents managed the situation at home, we're left to figure out what, if anything, his parents can do to help him work through the challenges he now faces. To be candid, Omar's parents are quite limited in their role at this point in the story and can simply enforce limits on his purchases of technology, data plan usage, etc., assuming they are paying for part or all of these costs. Otherwise, this situation is up to Omar to face himself, potentially with the help and support of his roommate and others who care about him and who can talk with him about his excessive use of technology.

We purposely took Omar's story into the first term in college to illustrate that his parents' role in influencing him once in college is limited, and they will need to have enough trust in Omar and his university to work through the consequences and solutions. Given the path that Omar is on, it's likely that his grades, personal relationships, and health will suffer due to his excessive technology use, and his parents will need to allow those consequences to run their course, as painful as that sounds. We realize we haven't tied Omar's story into a nice bow with a happy ending, but that's often the reality of the college student experience as he encounters failures, successes, hardships, accomplishments, and all of the other elements of this transitionary time towards adulthood.

Parent-Student Conversation Starters

Use these questions to get the conversation going with your student. Revisit them regularly throughout your student's high school and early college career:

- What do you do to manage your technology use? How can we as a family help you create balance?
- Do you know anyone who seems to have an unhealthy relationship with technology? What does that look like?
- What do you use technology for? How has it helped you complete tasks?

- What would you do if you didn't have access to your phone or the Internet? How would you entertain yourself?

Parent Resources

Bauerlein, Mark. *The Dumbest Generation: How the Digital Age Stupefies Young Americans and Jeopardizes Our Future (Or, Don't Trust Anyone Under 30)*. Tarcher, 2008.

The provocative title would suggest that the book is simply a critical rant about young people, but it's really not. It's a data-driven analysis of the impact of technology on young people and their knowledge and learning with thoughtful discussion about potential remedies that parents and others can explore.

WHY WE LOVE IT: We want to make sure no parent is naïve about the potential negative impact of technology on student learning and success, and this book will shatter any of that!

~~~

Maushart, Susan. *Winter of Our Disconnect: How Three Totally Wired Teenagers (and a Mother Who Slept with Her iPhone) Pulled the Plug on Their Technology and Lived to Tell the Tale*. TarcherPerigee, 2011.

What happens when a mother of three teenagers decides to take six-month reprieve from smartphones and the Internet? It is not as explosive as you think! Although the author admits it wasn't easy for her or her kids, she describes how their lives and their everyday tasks changed without the advantage of a computer or

Wikipedia. Her family discovers interests and skills they wouldn't have found otherwise.

WHY WE LOVE IT: Who doesn't want to live vicariously through another family when they spend half a year living in a technology desert. With lots of heart and humor, Maushart provides readers with a personal glimpse of the trials and tribulations. Spoiler alert: They all survive!

A Final Note from the Authors

By now, you should have a good idea of the essential qualities, skills, and habits that a successful student in college can develop while she is still in high school. But we would be remiss if we didn't address something that we know sometimes nags at parents when they have a student who just doesn't seem to be on track for college after high school despite having developed most, if not all, college-readiness skills. The following paragraphs capture our take on what to do if you think your student may not be ready for college now or may not choose to attend directly after high school.

What If My High-School Student Isn't Ready for College?

Here's the quick and dirty truth: Not every student is prepared for, or even interested in, pursuing a traditional college degree upon graduating from high school, and that is okay. Parents are in the best position to make that determination in consultation with their student. If you and your student decide that college is not the appropriate next step, however, you still need to have a plan. There are jobs available for workers who have a high-school diploma or its equivalent, but, on average, these jobs tend to pay less and provide less job security compared to employment opportunities for workers with some post-high school technical certificates, an associate's degree from a community college, or a bachelor's degree from a college or university.

If you and your student decide that she's not going to pursue a college degree immediately after graduating high school, we recommend that you develop a plan, in writing, for how your student will still progress towards independent living at some point in time. How long will you allow her to live in your home? Will she be responsible for paying rent and other costs? What is her plan for employment? If she can't find a job, what types of technical training, certificates, or other post-high school educational opportunities will she pursue? Is military service a consideration? There are many viable options for high-school graduates who don't feel ready or who aren't interested in pursuing a bachelor's degree, and your student will need to explore those options and select one that will move her on the path towards independence. We are saying this with the assumption, of course, that you don't aspire to have a 26-year-old living under your roof in a few years! Some of these options include workforce development programs, outdoor leadership programs, technical schools, apprenticeships, and the military.

Our final thoughts are this: Regardless of where your student lands after high school and no matter her pathway, she will have the skills and the opportunities to refine those skills to be successful in whatever she chooses. You have been instrumental in that development, and no matter how well you have done to help her, she has the ability to demonstrate resilience and tenacity in pursuing whatever goals she chooses for herself.

Endnotes

[1] Csikszentmihalyi, Mihaly. *Flow: The Psychology of Optimal Experience.* Penguin, 2008. His TED Talk provides a good overview of the concept: https://www.ted.com/talks/mihaly_csikszentmihalyi_on_flow.

[2] Brooks, Katharine. *You Majored in What?: Mapping Your Path from Chaos to Career.* Plume, 2010. Her first few chapters give a good overview of the exploration process for finding a purpose. She includes activities that your student can complete to create a map of potential pathways for study and career choices.

[3] This thinking technique was originally developed by Sakichi Toyoda at the Toyota Motor Corporation as a process of problem solving.

[4] Duckworth, Angela. *Grit: The Power of Passion and Perseverance.* Scribner, 2016. In Chapter 8: Purpose, Duckworth describes the research that points to the importance of developing a sense of purpose, or working at something that benefits as others, as a way to build resilience.

[5] Dweck, Carol. *Mindset: The New Psychology of Success.* Ballatine, 2007.

[6] Smilkstein, Rita. *We're Born to Learn: Using the Brain's Natural Process to Create Today's Curriculum.* 2nd ed. Corwin, 2011.

[7] Duckworth's TED Talk can be found here: https://www.ted.com/talks/angela_lee_duckworth_grit_the_power_of_passion_and_perseverance. Her book *Grit* devotes an entire chapter to the concept of deliberate practice.

[8] Duckworth, Angela. *Grit: The Power of Passion and Perseverance.* Scribner, 2016.

[9] Dweck explains the power of "yet" in this video: https://www.greatschools.org/gk/videos/parenting-tips-power-of-yet-carol-dweck-video/

[10] Duckworth, Angela. *Grit: The Power of Passion and Perseverance.* Scribner, 2016.

[11] Dweck, Carol. *Mindset: The New Psychology of Success.* Ballatine, 2007.

[12] Duckworth, Angela. *Grit: The Power of Passion and Perseverance.* Scribner, 2016. p. 138.

[13] Fine, Debra. *Beyond Texting: The Fine Art of Face-to-Face Communication for Teenagers.* Cannon Publishers, 2014.

[14] Stone, Douglas, Patton, Bruce, and Heen, Sheila. *Difficult Conversations: How to Discuss What Matters Most.* Penguin, 2010.

[15] Conley, David. *College Knowledge: What It Really Takes for Students to Succeed and What We Can Do to Get Them Ready.* Jossey-Bass, 2008. pp. 76-77.

[16] StrengthsQuest 2.0 information can be found at the website: http://www.strengthsquest.com/home.aspx.

[17] Fleming, Neil. VARK® Learning Styles Questionnaire: http://vark-learn.com/.

[18] Duckworth's Grit Scale can be found here: http://angeladuckworth.com/grit-scale/.

[19] Hazard, Laurie L. and Nadeau, Jean-Paul. *Foundations for Learning: Claiming Your Education*, 3rd ed. Pearson Education, 2011

[20] For more information about the adolescent brain, check out this information: http://hrweb.mit.edu/worklife/youngadult/brain.html.

[21] The American College Health Association survey information was reported in the following *Wall Street Journal* article: https://www.wsj.com/articles/college-counselors-go-where-the-students-aredorms-and-starbucks-1499631617.

9 781629 671154